The Startup Hats
By David Gardner

The Startup Hats

Master the Many Roles of the Entrepreneur

The stuff I wish someone had told me
...and things I was told but didn't hear

The Startup Hats\ David Gardner

www.thestartuphats.com

ISBN: 978-0692313121

TO MY DAD

who said that I could do anything

AND TO MY MOM

who always added...if you read the right books first

Contents

Introduction

With degrees in philosophy and ancient languages, I have often said that the best thing my higher education did was to provide me with absolutely no marketable skills. I don't say this in jest. The reality is that had I graduated with a marketable degree, the odds are that I would have immediately gotten a job, gotten a mortgage, and lived out the rest of my days without ever considering starting my own ventures. Since no one would hire me, I stumbled into entrepreneurship simply as a means to service a mountain of student loan debt.

Over the last twenty-five years, I've had the privilege (... and sometimes heartache) of founding or co-founding multiple technology companies. I've also invested in and advised dozens of other startups ranging from enterprise software platforms to breweries. I've made plenty of mistakes, arrogantly blown a couple of potentially huge exits, and occasionally sold at just the right time. I was fortunate enough to have seven of my own startups successfully acquired in a row. The largest sold for $100 million in cash and the briefest lasted only eleven months before being acquired for $12 million.

Don't worry. This is not going to be about me. It's really about you and your venture. The last thing we need is another academic textbook or one of those auto-boast-agraphies where each chapter begins with some variation on "and then my brilliance was further demonstrated by..." In fact, I don't think I'm even a good role model. I did almost everything wrong for way too long before eventually figuring it out, always learning my lessons the hard way. To this day, I have no excuse for the generously given wisdom that languished at my doorstep.

So why should you listen to me? Most of you that are arrogant enough to think you know enough to defy the odds and build your own successful venture from the ground up, are probably a lot like I was in those early days. You should listen to me, not because I'm great or wise, but because I vividly remember every self-discovered truth and painful lesson endured. You should listen to me because I have a good memory, I'm honest, and I sincerely want to see every entrepreneur succeed. You should listen to me because; unfortunately *experience* gives you the test and then the lesson.

This book isn't about me, but it would be helpful for you to know a little something about how I became an entrepreneur. Being the first person to obtain a degree from either side of my family, I received little guidance concerning majors or career options when I headed off to college. I assumed that everyone studied whatever subjects they found most interesting without a thought to its marketability or income potential. For me this was history, ancient languages, and philosophy.

I had no money saved for college, but thankfully student loans were readily available. I finished my undergraduate in three years by taking heavy class loads that always exceeded twenty credit hours per semester while working nearly full time. This was simply a matter of economics for me. In those days, full time students paid the same amount regardless of whether they took twelve credit hours or twenty, so why not take twenty to save the cost of a full year of college? In hindsight, although this was good economics, I forfeited much of the college experience never to be relived. This was my first lesson in how things can look great in theory, but not play out so well in practice.

After graduating, I started a Master's of Divinity program at Southeastern Seminary and completely by accident discovered a love for computers. I wanted to write my thesis in ancient Greek, but there was a requirement that it be typed. Typewriters for dead language are in obvious short supply, but I had heard of something called a "word processor" that might enable me to accomplish this task. I took advantage of a special sale going on at the bookstore and purchased an IBM® portable PC. I learned that "portable" can be a very subjective term! This monster was the size of a suitcase and twice as heavy. It had no hard drive, only a 360K five-inch floppy drive, and a built-in six-inch amber monochrome monitor.

In those days IBM® shipped every computer with full documentation, which in this case included, a DOS operating manual, a BASIC® programming language manual, and floppy disks. Once I found the on switch, it booted up in the BASIC interpreter screen and the curser began mocking me. I opened the BASIC-programming manual to the first page, which fortunately happened to explain a BASIC command called "BEEP". So I typed in the letters "B-E-E-P" and pressed the return key. I will never forget my excitement as I heard a distinctive beep sound come from its little speaker stuck to the side of its humming power supply! My eyes widened at this unexpected epiphany, "*...you can tell it to do stuff?*"

I began experimenting with other commands, IF-THEN statements, GOTO statements, and FOR-NEXT loops. My mind raced with excitement, as the possibilities with this machine suddenly seemed endless. Before long I was drawing graphical objects on the screen. I would erase and re-draw them so as to create the illusion of things flying around in space. For no reason, I began writing my first big program, a spaceship game. It would be considered amazingly simplistic by today's standards, but in the early eighties, the state of the industry was a black and white 2D ping-pong ball bouncing back and forth between line paddles. I began reading computer hobbyists' magazines to pick up coding tips. I even figured out how to install more memory and a second floppy drive so I could compile my code without having to laboriously switch floppy disks dozens of times. Let's be honest, my code was horrible. If I had had even a rudimentary understanding of calculus at the time I could have replaced pages of IF-THEN statements with a single equation, but it worked and it was really fun to play.

So I spent my days reading Nietzsche and Bonhoeffer and translating manuscripts, but in truth I couldn't wait to get back to my room and to the world I was creating on my little amber screen.

In those days, we called open source programs "shareware" which was comprised mostly of games and simple utility programs. I decided to send my game into one of the computer hobbyists magazine publishers for review. A few weeks later, I received a letter in the mail. I will never forget my second computer epiphany as I read the letter. They wanted to include my program on one of the shareware floppy disks that were distributed inside of their magazine *AND* they were willing me pay me for it! My eyes widened again, "*...you can make money doing this?*"

As soon as the semester was over, I enrolled at North Carolina State University. My goal was to complete a master's degree in information science, but I had a lot of remedial math and science classes to make up. Although it was difficult, it was very refreshing to see right and wrong answers on tests rather than just essay questions regarding the conflicting opinions of others.

I was making ends meet by writing simple programs for small local businesses. I developed several custom point-of-sale and inventory control applications. At that time, an information technology solution was very comprehensive. I would write the code, build the computers from mail ordered parts, and even set up the local area network before training the staff and providing them with on-going support. I read a lot of manuals. The great thing in those days was that you didn't have to know much to look like a real genius because very few people even owned a computer or understood software's potential for transforming their business.

By the end of my second year at NCSU, I had invoiced over a million dollars and found myself predominately hiring other students to do most of the work. I rented some space in a small strip mall and started a computer store. A year later, at six million in revenue and twenty-seven employees, I dropped out of my third year at NCSU thinking it was better to make payroll than to do homework assignments.

I sold my computer store and began working with a friend to build a project based software-only development company. Computer hardware margins were heading south, but the client-server computing model was in full swing. Companies were moving applications off of their mainframes and onto more cost-effective and user-friendly personal computers. Over the next few years I sold, designed, and managed literally hundreds of custom software development projects predominately for Fortune 1000 companies. My teams developed the very first customer banking application for BB&T® and a massive admissions system for Duke® University. We wrote the equivalent of salesforce.com® at least six times for different clients! You think it would have occurred to me that there was a product to be made here, but when you are in a services mindset, it is very hard to think beyond the next project.

I did not appreciate it at the time, but I now realize how this services-based company exposed me to almost every industry and aspect of business. From manufacturing lines and sales force automation to part eleven compliant pharmaceutical document tracking, we were cranking out the code as fast as we could go. In a few short years, we had grown to nearly two hundred employees.

Although custom projects were fun and lucrative, I did slowly began to realize what all small services-based companies learn; if I were to ever stop working as hard as I was working, the revenue would dry up. The companies that could scale up quickly and get huge exit multiples were the ones with intellectual property i.e. *products*. It became clear to me that I needed to stop developing software for hire and start building my own products. Fortunately, working daily with dozens of chief information officers and IT managers had put me in a good position to recognize which new software product offerings might have the most potential and demand.

I spent the next few decades founding software product companies. Each of the startups I founded was in a different industry. From human resources, to healthcare, to education, I loved designing transformational software to solve business problems. I was utterly fascinated by how unique each market segment and sales cycle was. Business for me was like an enjoyable puzzle. At first, I thought that all I had to do was design products that would create the right value propositions to solve the most painful problems I could discover. There was so much more I needed to know about business, people and myself. Unfortunately, I wasn't a great listener so I had to learn most of my lessons the hard way.

Starting companies is not for the faint of heart. No matter how much you love what you do, consistently working twelve and fifteen-hour days will take a toll on you. When I sold my last company, I promised my wonderful and patient wife that I would never again start my own venture.

Throughout my career, no matter how busy I was with my own ventures, I tried to always take the time to speak with new entrepreneurs seeking advice. I saw it as my duty and something that was owed because of those who had helped me along the way. So when I retired from starting my own ventures, I began to focus all of my energy on mentoring young entrepreneurs. Local entrepreneurs came to know me as the advisor who consulted for merely a coffee or beer. It is not an exaggeration to say that literally hundreds of entrepreneurs have sat on my back deck, overlooking my lake, while discussing their go-to-market strategy, staffing problems, and other startup issues.

Although every venture is unique, I found myself giving certain advice over and over again and hearing back how beneficial it was. I encapsulated some of this guidance into a short document to share with new entrepreneurs mainly as a time saver. It really surprised me how popular that document became as entrepreneurs began sharing it with each other and discussing it among themselves. Several entrepreneurs, angel investors, and venture capitalists, have encouraged me to expand on that document and make it available to a wider audience. This book is my effort to shortcut your learning process as an entrepreneur.

If you have the time and money to complete an MBA, I am sure that you would learn a lot more than I can communicate here, but if you do not, then you may find this book a very practical summary of what I found most important when starting a venture. If you already have an MBA or business experience, you may still find what I have to say very practical. In my experience, it's not the stuff we don't know that screws us up in life, but all the stuff we did learn, but yet somehow forgot to implement. I specifically focus on software business-to-business (B2B) startups, but most of this book is applicable to business-to-consumer (B2C) and non-software related ventures as well.

Unlike most professions that require you to wear only one hat really well, successful entrepreneurship dictates that you wear multiple hats all reasonably well. In fact, your typical day will be a flurry of putting on and taking off your diverse hats each encompassing a role you must fulfill in order for your startup to not only survive, but also thrive. Depending on your strengths and personality, you will gravitate towards and feel more comfortable with some hats than others, but ignore any of them at your peril.

You will notice that each of the hats discussed here can also be viewed as a stage or step in building your startup. Each step rests upon and is dependent on the ones that came before it. In a startup you rarely have the luxury of choosing which hats you want to wear or spend time under. You have to wear them all and to short change one hat is likely to sabotage them all.

If you are an aspiring entrepreneur living by your wits, taking the leaps of faith, dodging the bullets and clenching relentlessly to your dream, then I want you to know that my respect for you is immense and this book is truly all about you. I think people, who aren't a little scared every morning when they wake up, are at best unchallenged and at worst not fully alive. Whether you succeed or fail is not nearly as important as the fact that you experienced the journey. If you embrace it, your venture will shape you even as you are shaping it. I hope this book serves you well on your journey.

The Entrepreneur Hat

After speaking on entrepreneurship at a conference a few years ago, I was taking questions from the audience when a wide-eyed young man near the front raised his hand. He asked what arguably might be the two best questions any would-be entrepreneur should ask, "How do I know if I'm cut out to be an entrepreneur and what is it like to start your own company?" I said that starting a new venture is a rush full of stress and uncertainty, but one that will get you out of bed excited to get going every morning. You put together a little pot of money against a plan that you honestly don't know will work and then you try like hell to get cash flow in the positive before your dollars run out. It's like jumping out of an airplane without a parachute; all you have is a bag full of really ambitious silk worms and you are knitting as fast as you can all of the way down!

The first hat is the entrepreneur's hat. If it doesn't fit well then none of the other required hats will either. Unlike the other hats that basically represent skill sets, the entrepreneur's hat is more of an attitude or personality type. There are many life experiences that are a must-have for some people, but would be a tragedy for others. It all comes down to what makes you happy, yet at the same time makes you crazy. Even if you manage to get your company going and make money, if you are miserable every day of that process then this is not what I would call "being successful".

The first thing I do when coaching a new entrepreneur is to help that person discover if this is what he or she really wants. An old Chinese *curse* reads, "May you get what you want". Most people believe that startups fail because the entrepreneur lacks the required skills. Although this can certainly contribute to failure, I believe the main reason is that many of these people were not entrepreneurs at the core and simply decided it was time to stop being miserable.

If you are thinking about being an entrepreneur you should start by asking yourself, "What energizes me? What gets you excited and makes you want to work harder than you've ever worked before? Does risk intrigue you or repel you? Are you happiest when everything is neatly organized and in its place or when options are flying round with unlimited possibilities and potential?"

One thing I can tell you with certainty is that a start up is chaos. A bird only gets off the ground and flies if it flaps its wings feverishly. There is a burst of activity that comes from all directions as you get your company going. Founding a startup means rarely getting to complete a full train of thought, at least not in one sitting. On many occasions, in the midst of starting a new venture, I have begun an email in the morning and not finished it until late that night. Before I could finish it the phone rings, a text message comes in, emails and chat messages pop up, and people would walk into my office needing immediate decisions.

Some people thrive on such chaos. They enjoy the diversity of the day and the struggle to slowly bring order to the mayhem. They aren't overwhelmed by a need to get to the bottom of their in-box each day. They actually find the turbulent process invigorating like a brisk run on a cold day. They get satisfaction at the end of the day in knowing that they fought well that day even if no milestone was achieved. A startup is not a hockey game where one giant score wins the day. It is a football game where success is measured in inches as you fight for each precious yard.

If you need to have everything organized and in its proper place before you can call it a night, then the startup world is probably not for you. Successful entrepreneurs are always organizing. They keep a to-do list, but are perpetually reprioritizing it, demoting a handful of items, delegating some, and just doing enough to get by on others because that's all the time they merit at the moment. This is more than multi-tasking. It's making up rules and processes while you play. If you can't get comfortable with chaos, entrepreneurship is probably going to kill you or at least leave you longing for that predictable corporate job you abandoned.

Besides being at peace with chaos, entrepreneurs are also known for their work ethic. Do you feel cheated after a hard day's work that ran longer than expected and cut into your free time or do you arrive home with a feeling of extra accomplishment? Starting your own venture will probably be the most difficult thing you'll ever do. You will work harder than you have ever worked, but if entrepreneurship runs in your veins then it won't really feel like it does when you work hard for someone else. Another good definition of an entrepreneur is a person who is so crazy that she or he will work seventy hours per week for themselves just to avoid working forty hours a week for anyone else! When the line between your work and leisure starts to blur and you don't really care then you might just be an entrepreneur.

The root word from which the word *business* is derived is "busy". Your inbox will never be empty; not even close to empty because there is always more you could and should be doing. You will be perpetually understaffed and doing the job of three people because you can't yet afford to hire the staff you need. Even if you could, you'd struggle to find the time to train and manage them.

Your small team will be watching you as you unknowingly create a culture that expects and prides itself on working hard and working fast. A candidate interviewing at one of my startups once asked me if we allowed employees to work from home to which I replied, "Certainly...at night and on weekends!" I've always said that a startup really does have the most flexible work hours of all because you get to choose any seventy hours per week that fits your schedule the best!

So why would anyone choose to work this hard and deal with this much stress? When you are captain of your own ship, charting your own course each day and deciding how to spend your time, tremendous creativity and satisfaction are abundant. When people are free to create, it releases a seemingly boundless energy that's almost impossible to find at large companies among the rank and file. Workers in conglomerates tend to find themselves in a pigeonhole with well-established policies, procedures & permission processes that, although necessary, can drain away precious creativity and energy. A life in the ranks can certainly offer more security and predictability but not what most would consider adventure. To get adventure, you have to have the high-risk and high-reward that's not typically in the cards for the vast majority of corporate automatons. If the unknown and uncertain calls out to you, then again you might just be an entrepreneur.

Finally, with very few exceptions, the successful entrepreneurs I know are all good to great sales people who have made peace with the necessity of perpetually selling. Most of them really enjoy making their case and convincing others of the merits of their arguments. I've heard a lot of would-be entrepreneurs tell me, "I'm not a sales person." To this I typically respond, "Then you are probably not an entrepreneur." Every successful entrepreneur is at least competent at sales. You might be a brilliant engineer, who has created a far better mousetrap, but the fact remains that it is not the better mousetrap that usually win. Instead it is the entrepreneur who can persuade everyone that he or she has a mousetrap for sale with significantly more benefits than they really want and need.

There's no getting around it. If you are starting a company then you are going to spend perhaps the largest part of your day under the sales hat. You are going to be selling investors on how your venture is going to make them a good return. You are going to be selling the best candidates on why they should work for your little startup. You are going to be selling those first few critically important prospects on why they should take a chance on you. And then, when you screw up, you are going to be selling the customers you've disappointed on why they should continue to believe in you and give you another chance. Indeed, the sales hat is one you never truly get to hand off for very long. Even when your company grows to hundreds or even thousands of sales professionals, when the deal is big, the damage unthinkable or the account critical, you are going to be once again drafted into sales. So if you just can't see yourself doing the job of a salesperson then find a partner who lives for it or seriously rethink your foray into entrepreneurship.

Still think you are an entrepreneur? Then the next question is *when*. When should you take that leap? I talk to many would-be entrepreneurs struggling with their desire to take on the high risk of a new venture because they are addicted to their current income level and lifestyle. It gets even harder when others depend on your income as a provider because even if you are willing to take risks yourself, is it fair that they should have to risk so much as well? Starting a company in this situation becomes a family discussion and a family commitment because everyone has to be willing to sign on in order to be successful.

It is usually easiest to start your venture when you are young, broke, and single, but I've worked with several middle aged and even older entrepreneurs that succeeded wonderfully. Sometimes they have a nest egg they are ready to gamble while others figure out ways to de-risk their venture by getting a long way down the field before they give up their day job. A lot of startup incubators will not assist someone who is still employed. They will tell you that you aren't serious until you quit your day job. I very much disagree. Some of my most successful entrepreneurs engineered ways to minimize the risk associated with their ventures. You can design a lot of software at night and on weekends. You can organize focus groups and test your assumptions. You can recruit and sell on a contingency basis. My advice is delay the start of your capital burn for as long as possible.

So. If you think that you might be an entrepreneur and that the time for your venture might be upon you...then keep reading.

There is another personality type that I've seen struggle with entrepreneurship; the *perfectionist*. Startups are usually not the place where we have the opportunity to get things perfect or even try to do so. We generally do things just well enough and then move on. In other words, time is our most precious commodity so I encourage entrepreneurs to be very stingy with it. Since that last 10% often doubles the time commitment, it is usually not a good deal for entrepreneurs to have a constant backlog. This thinking is contrary to the thinking of most corporate workers. In a big company you most often want to do a project as well as you possibly can even if the last 10% costs you twice as much time as the entire project. It is the quality of the final deliverable upon which you are usually evaluated and promoted.

I have found that those from healthcare and engineering backgrounds, for example, particularly struggle with the "good enough" concept. All of their training has been around a zero-mistake mentality. I'm glad that medical doctors and bridge builders think this way, but when it comes to a startup, that mentality can drain your venture dry. A common stereotype among investors is that doctors are horrible businessmen. I did not understand this since doctors are some of the smartest and hardest working people I know, but after helping some with their startups I came to see that it was their perfectionism that most often was keeping them from achieving the speed that startups require. They are very comfortable under the construction hat, but they wear it way too long and starve their ventures of the time so desperately needed from the other required hats.

Successful entrepreneurs think in terms of opportunity costs because their time is so precious. They know that they could polish that PowerPoint® for another hour and perhaps make it 5% better, but this would be at the cost of not getting two other important tasks done that day. For most startups the goal is not perfection, but efficiency and good enough is almost always better than flawless in a startup. If that last sentence sticks in your claw then you may not be an entrepreneur.

Business consultant and thinker, Tom Peters, calls this concept "falling forward fast". Shamefully, I was on my third startup before I came to fully understand what he was talking about. In a startup you will be dealing with a bunch of unproven assumptions and unknowns. There is a stumbling about as we try things, see what works, throw out the plan or revise the plan and try again. Peters argues that we should encourage our workers to make all of the mistakes they can as quickly as possible because this is how we learn what works. In the purest sense, a startup is fast experimentation and iteration on an ever-evolving hypothesis. Obviously, if what we are working on so diligently might have to get replaced or significantly modified in the near future then it makes no sense to polish it unto perfection. There will be a time for polishing, but not until you are very close to 100% confident that you have nailed it and by then they probably won't still be calling your venture a startup anymore.

We often build a prototype that is just good enough to give customers a concept so that they can give us feedback. We quickly modify a click-through agreement knowing that it will need to be replaced by a real lawyer once we get a lot of customers, but it's "good enough" for now. If no one buys this then the agreement is pointless anyway, so put in a "good-enough" placeholder and keep moving. Stick and move. Stick and move. Switch hats. Circle back when necessary. This is life in a startup.

I guess it's a little unusual to start a book on entrepreneurship by trying to talk the reader out of becoming an entrepreneur but that might be some of the best advice you'll ever receive. I met an executive at a party a few months ago. He seemed to know me and just started talking. I asked him if I had helped him with a venture. He said that we sat and talked on my back deck about ten years earlier and that I had helped him discover that he did not want to be an entrepreneur. He smiled, "Best advice I have ever received."

Ah, but some of you are still reading. You are undaunted by my less-than-glorified portrait of life in a startup. In fact, you found it exhilarating. The rest of this book is for you so open up your closet and let's try on some of the hats that you are going to need.

The Navigator's Hat

Wouldn't it be great if entrepreneurs could see into the future? We'd know which ventures to avoid and which ones will really pay off. We'd know how much money we were going to need and when. We'd be prepared for whatever was waiting for us around the next bend.

Starting a new venture is a lot like being Magellan or one of those early explorers sailing out into the unknown. It's the unknown part of the equation that creates the adventure's excitement and risk. Several of those early explorers didn't make it back. I don't remember their names because history kind of forgot about them. The successful one's that we do remember didn't just jump into a boat and hope for the best. Those explorers spent months, sometime years, planning and preparing for their journey. How big of a ship will I need? How much food? How will I deal with storms? What will the winds and current be like? And most important, what course is best?

The great explorers were good sailors, but so were the guys who drowned and starved. What made explorers successful was their ability to plan and navigate. Hope is never a strategy. Long before they stood majestically posed on the bow of their ship, they spent countless hours hunched over candles, thinking through every possibility scenario they might encounter. Those early navigators made best-guest assumptions about riggings, food consumption, wind and current patterns, and modified those assumptions each day as new data was collected. They were great explorers first and foremost because they were great planners.

Successful entrepreneurs don't just jump in the water and start swimming. Like the Boy Scout mantra says, they were always prepared. The navigator's hat is one of the very first hats you have to put on as an entrepreneur. If your plan is not sound, then you really won't have a business at all. Planning or *modeling* a new venture as accurately as possible provides the insights needed to successfully surf the edge between growing your venture as fast as possible and not running out of money. It is the tool that will help you understand your costs and what resources you'll need. More than any other document, it is also going to give potential investors insights into how their money will be used to generate a return and the confidence they need to put up the seed capital you need.

Knowing how to use a spreadsheet is a must. As precious as the early navigator's compass and sexton, it is your spreadsheet that makes navigation for your venture possible. If you aren't comfortable modeling things over time using a spreadsheet then I'd suggest you stop reading this and go learn. It's not that hard, but it is an imperative skill. There are very few businesses today that can be managed without a solid spreadsheet model and someone at the helm who knows how to use it to steer.

The Startup Hats

Business modeling is a little bit of predictive science and a lot of educated best guessing. I like to build a model on the first spreadsheet tab that shows sections for forecasted revenue, costs, and cash-on-hand over consecutive months projected across the horizontal axis. These go out two to three years based on assumptions that are listed in the first two columns as seen in the next image. Try not to hardwire numbers under each month that might change, but rather have them calculate automatically from a formula based on the assumption you are making to the left. This way, you can modify an assumption and the forecasted row to the right of it recalculates automatically. In your revenue section, for example, you might show the number of salespeople you plan to have each month. How many sales they will make and at what price points are all calculated from the assumptions listed at the beginning of each row.

	A	B	C	D	E	F	G	H	I
1	Assumptions			Projections					
2					14-Sep	14-Oct	14-Nov	14-Dec	14-Jan
3	Revenue Assumptions			REVENUE					
4	Revenue Assumption 1	4.0		Sales Made					
5	Revenue Assumption 2	$450.00		Price per Sale					
6	Revenue Assumption 3	3.70%		Recurring Customers					
7				Total Revenue					
8	Expense Assumptions			EXPENSES					
9	Cost of Goods Sold	$66.57							
10	Labor Cost								
11	Salary 1	$25,000		Job title 1					
12	Salary 2	$55,000		Job title 2					
13	Contractor	$25,000		R&D Contractors					
14	Marketing Cost 1	$33		Channel 1					
15	Marketing Cost 2	$500		Advertising					
16	Commissions	7.80%		Commissions					
17	G&A Expense Assumptions								
18	Professsional Services	$500		Professsional Services					
19	Credit Card Processing Fee	2.80%		Credit Card Fees					
20	Office	$2,000		Rent					
21	Software Licenses	$150		Software					
22	Web Hosting	$75		Hosting Service					
23	Hardware	$500		Hardware					
24				Total Expenses					
25				CASH FLOW					
26				Revenue					
27				All Costs					
28				Profit					
29									
30	Starting Cash	$250,000		Cash on Hand					

This example is very simplistic and used here only to show a proposed organizational layout. Your model may have revenue sources with specific associated costs. I like this layout because it keeps the assumptions in line with the variables they modify. Most importantly, it keeps those critically important assumptions up front, forcing entrepreneurs to constantly re-evaluate them.

An assumption is anything that you might be wrong about or that might change as you try to forecast the most likely future of your business. Assumptions are things like the price you think your customer will pay, deal size, how much you will need to pay your staff, how many marketing dollars you will have to spend to acquire a new customer, and/or how many sales your average sales person can make in a month. Some models have a few dozen assumptions while others can have hundreds. Don't get one of those elaborate spreadsheet templates with dozens of tabs that will take you months to understand. Build your own. Start simple. Model only the most salient features and variable that will most dramatically affect your venture.

First, you need to acknowledge what you don't know. What are the variables that will affect your business? There are many great discussions that this exercise generates around costs, sales cycle, customer churn, receivables/collection time, when to hire, etc. For all practical purposes, this spreadsheet forecast is your business. It is the steering wheel on your ship, without which, you are just waiting for monthly financials and guessing. All of the numbers in a given month's column are added or subtracted as necessary to produce the cash-on-hand number at the bottom of that column. This number is like the EKG bleep on a heart monitor. If it goes negative then your venture will most likely die on that date.

Next, hunt down reasonable starting assumptions for the variables in your model. This can be difficult, but you have to start with at least reasonable assumptions based on what you can know now.

I was recently working with a startup that wanted to sell HVAC air filters online via a consumer subscription model. A little research into shipping rates was all it took to come up with a reasonable assumption as to what their typical box shipping costs might be, but they also needed to know less obvious things, such as how often will consumers feel it is necessary to change their home air filters. They also needed to know things like what percentage of their customers would purchase the really cheap filters versus the more expensive and higher margin hypoallergenic filters. Both of these numbers would dramatically affect their forecasted revenue, profit, and the amount of money they needed to raise.

Sometimes, you can get reasonable starting assumptions from a proxy. A proxy is a mature company or proven model that is similar in some way to parts of your new venture. One the companies I am advising offers a tablet-based customer comment card for services-based businesses like restaurants to obtain customer satisfaction survey data. When trying to forecast what a restaurant owner might be willing to pay for such a tool, they were able to find similar offerings such as web-based surveys offered to customers via URL addresses printed on their cash register receipt. Although not a one-to-one comparison, it did give them a reasonable data point as to how valuable restaurateurs considered this type of tool and in effect, what they might be willing to pay for something similar.

Sometimes you just have to be clever and diligent to get the data points you need. The subscription service filter guys needed to model a number for what their warehouse shipping clerks were going to cost each month. We were able to research help wanted ads to find out the typical salary range for shipping clerks. To find out how often consumers change their filters, they could have just hung out at Lowes® or Home Depot® in the air filter isle and asked the people picking up filters how long it has been since their last filter change.

Even a small sampling can give you a feel for a reasonable starting number for an assumption. I am a big believer in focus groups. Invite a bunch of people over for pizza and ask them to critique your reasoning. Have them take a survey and average your findings. So long as the group you are pulling from is representative of your demographic, you should be able to at least get a starting number. Be careful not to lead your audience into telling you what they think you want to hear. And be mindful of how you word survey questions. Often, you can get very different results simply by wording a question in a slightly different way, insinuating different connotations.

The Startup Hats

In <u>The Art of War</u>, Sun Tzu said that no battle plan survives the first arrow. I'm not a big fan of a detailed written business plans, which always seems obsolete a month after it is written, but I'm a huge fan of a detailed spreadsheet model; a living document where the logic behind every number can be explained in detail and updated as needed. You can do a polished written plan if you choose, but those with the scars from many hands-on startup battles will tell you that in the early days, it is best to save your precious time for the spreadsheet model.

By "living document", I mean that the model is always being updated. I encourage entrepreneurs to establish the discipline each month of overwriting the forecasted cell equations for that month with the real actual data. Once you have the real number of sales for the month of March, you should overwrite the forecasting equations in these cells with the actual sales number. Then look to see if your assumption to the left should be updated in light of the new actual data point. For example, you may have assumed that an inside sales person would close four sales per week, but for the last two months you notice that they have on average only closed 2.3 sales. Modifying the variable "average sales closed per month per sales person" from 4.0 to 2.3 will recalculate your model for all future months. Now, how does your model look? What changes might you need to implement based on your new forecasted future?

Your forecast is like your radar telling you about both problems and opportunities you are likely to face in the future. You will find that certain assumptions are not that critical, but others can dramatically change your outcome. These are the ones you need to pay very close attention to, run what-if scenarios on and have a few contingency plans in your pocket. I like to include a graph at the bottom of my model that shows dollars on the vertical axis and months across the horizontal. Only three lines are graphed; gross revenue, total expenses and cash-on-hand. Where the revenue and expense line cross in the future, is where your venture reaches that important cash flow positive state. The cash line will be dropping rapidly each month until your revenue number exceeds your expense line. If you've raised enough startup capital and you have a viable business model, then the cash-on-hand line will not go into the negative.

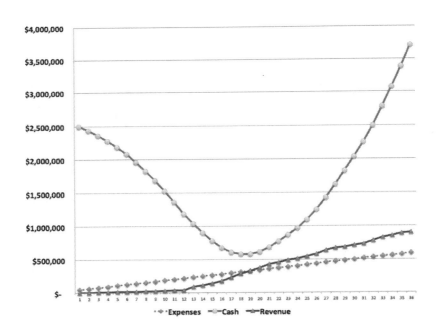

Over time your spreadsheet model can become amazingly accurate at predicting the future. I sometimes refer to a mature model as a "crystal ball". Keep in mind that accurate modeling is useless unless you are willing to make the hard decisions necessary based on the information and forecasts it provides. Sometimes the model will encourage you to be more aggressive with new hires and marketing, while other times it will warn you to proceed with a slower and more cautious approach. Any business can have a stellar or down month so avoid making knee jerk decisions, but when a pattern emerges, it is the navigator's job to act decisively. Don't hesitate to downsize if that's what it takes to keep your venture afloat. And don't procrastinate doing what you know needs to be done by saying each month that you can make it up next month. Saying, "We can sell our way out of this" is akin to the proverbial redneck saying, "Watch this". Something bad usually happens next. It's easy to dig a hole that you can't climb out of. As an entrepreneur, your forecast is your best friend, but it is only as good as your commitment to act on it. If the radar tells you there is an iceberg ahead and you ignore the information, then there's no real benefit to having radar in the first place.

I believe that it is very important to develop your business model yourself. Don't hand this task off to your accountant or rented CFO. You need to do this yourself because you need to understand your business and building this model yourself is the best way for you to accomplish that. It will also empower you to interpret what the model is telling you in the future. If you can't model your business yourself on a computer screen, then there's no way you are going to be able to build it in the real world.

I'll close out this section with a few practical tips to remember when building your model. First, be conservative. I love how entrepreneurs tend to be optimists. As children, I'm certain that had we been put in pool of horse manure up to our necks we simply would have smiled and looked for a pony to ride. Normally optimism is a good thing, but the one occasion when it will work against you is forecasting. I have found most first-pass revenue models to be overstated by 100%. So if the range for estimated sales is 3 to 7 per month, then use 3 sales per month or better yet, 2 sales per month as the assumption in your model. Being ahead of plan is a wonderful problem to have, but finding yourself overextended and undercapitalized is as horrible psychologically as it is fiscally. You also don't want to set expectations for your investors that aren't realistic. Investment terms often give your investors the rights to take more equity, decline a promised capital call, or even to fire you from your own company if you get too far behind plan. So don't hand out big sticks that might be used later on in your beating.

When doing your initial model, keep an open mind. If conservative numbers just don't work, then don't hesitate to walk away from your idea or to radically change the plan. Many great ideas are just not practical, can't be monetized or require more startup capital then you will be able to attract. Success is much more about the entrepreneur than the idea so don't get all emotionally attached to your first love. The model did its job so you can now free up your time and your mind for the next more viable idea.

Second, develop your model on a *cash* basis rather than an *accrual* basis. This simply means that when you make a sale; don't recognize the revenue until you have actually received it. Some businesses are credit card based and you get the money at the time of the sales transaction. However others, especially most B2B sales, will be on NET 30 to even NET 60 terms. This leaves you waiting a month or two to get paid. Even if your accounting system is accrual based, your model should always be cash based because if you can't make payroll, your employees aren't really going to care that you have lots of theoretical cash on the books. This often means modeling the revenue a month or two after the sale, which can make a big difference in how much money you need to raise or keep on hand.

A startup is all about not running out of money, so focus on the left side of your graph i.e. the months prior to the revenue and expense line crossing. This is the area that is critically important to monitor and manage. These graphs often hockey stick up towards the right side and that is a wonderful thing, but that is not where you must focus. Obviously, if you were netting half a million per month in profits, then your plan would change radically. While that may be great, you have to survive the lean months or even years to the left of that graphical intersection. Therefore, manage on the left side of the revenue-expense intersection or you may never get to the right side.

Keep your expense lines as minimal as possible. The trappings of business are just distractions that shorten your runway. Unless you are a customer destination center, you don't need fine desks or bookcases. Flex space and folding tables are often more than enough to get you going. A true entrepreneur would trade his or her nice desk any day to fund one additional marketing campaign in those early days. The tremendous amount of used office furniture and equipment available today is testament that most startups don't make it, especially the ones with fancy trappings. And whatever you do, avoid those $800 Aeron® chairs, even the used ones. I think they might be bad luck because every startup I've ever seen that had even just one ran out money!

Just like those early explorers sailing out into the abyss, you need to be armed with a well-conceived plan. Making high-risk decisions with limited information is scary and the main reason why the faint of heart don't start companies. However, a well-conceived and continuously updated business model will be the precious instrument panel that enables you to navigate your ship through the fog of an uncertain future.

The Banker's Hat

So you've completed your model! You've done your homework and feel good about your starting assumptions. You understand and are ready to defend your model/plan and you know how much starting capital you are going to need. Now, it's time to put on the banker's hat and go raise some money.

Many entrepreneurs at this point turn to friends and family for their initial capital. I'm not a big fan of this. Warren Buffet was once asked if losing his money on a venture was his worst-case scenario to which he responded, "No...it feels far worse to lose someone else's money". Nowhere is this truer than when it comes to family and friends. I encourage entrepreneurs raising capital to exhaust all other possible options first before turning to friends and family. The problem with friends and family money is that it's often just too easy to get. These investors typically aren't critical enough of your plan and don't really add anything to your venture other than capital. Furthermore, it's just not wise for them to make a single angel investment. Failure rates are very high in early stage ventures which is why angel investors diversify their portfolios, so it's pretty narcissistic (and selfish) to ask your friends and family to do something that more experienced investors are unwilling to do.

There are many reasons to first seek out seasoned individual angel investors, angel investment groups, and seed round venture capital funds. First of all, this gives you an opportunity to meet investors and potential advisors who may be able to provide much more than just capital to your venture. Second, if you are unable to persuade even one sophisticated investor into backing your venture, then you probably should seriously reevaluate your plan. These investors seek out promising opportunities and are willing to take larger risks. If you've talked to several and no one's interested, then I'd encourage you to seriously rethink your venture or at least the parts with which potential investors have concerns. Find out why they aren't interested. Maybe you've overlooked some critically important aspect. I'm not saying to give up...just rethink. Maybe you need to reposition your offer, target a different market, or raise a larger or smaller amount of capital. Don't just focus on *selling* potential investors. Approach them as potential advisors and ask them to challenge your reasoning and plan. Above all else, *listen*. This will serve you well and communicate that you are coachable... a character trait smart investors love to see.

Fund raising at any stage of your business can consume vast amounts of your time; time that could be used to grow your business organically. Venture capitalists (VCs) are the worst offenders when it comes to wasting your precious time. They are usually willing to meet with you so long as you cover your own travel costs. This is how they learn about new promising technologies and keep abreast of what's going on in various market sectors. Venture capitalists never sign non-disclosure agreements (NDAs) so there's always a chance that they might pick up something from you that could be beneficial to one of their portfolio companies. So, don't get too excited just because a VC agrees to meet with you.

The best way to make the inefficient process of fund raising as efficient as possible is to do your research. First, decide what type of investor you want to approach. Angel and angel groups are usually only good for small rounds i.e. under $500K. Venture capitalists fall into different categories depending on their size and the focus of their fund. A few will do very early stage, high risk, seed rounds but most limit these investments with strict criteria such as revenues above two million. Some funds are restricted to specific market sectors such as healthcare or clean energy technologies. A few will only invest in serial entrepreneurs with at least one successful exit behind them. If you fly up to meet with these guys and you're a first time jockey then you will have wasted precious time and capital.

Don't waste time trying to put your *round* company idea into a *square* funding hole. Break out your trusty spreadsheet and start a list of potential investors. There are various attributes you should include on your list as you decide which investors to approach. One of these variables is *proximity*. Some angel investors and all VCs like to stay involved in the ventures they back and they don't like to waste a lot of time traveling so the closer the investor is to where you are, or plan to be, the higher the probability of an investment. West coast VCs are known for being more aggressive than typical east coast VCs in investing in big ideas at earlier stages, but they hate flying to the east coast for board meetings. If you are on the West coast or willing to move your company there then your odds of getting an investment from these guys improves dramatically. If you fall into this category then west coast VC's, should be moved up on your spreadsheet.

Finding investors who have made money doing something similar to your proposed offering is another important criterion. Look over the portfolio companies listed on a VC's website. Is this firm investing in companies similar to yours? Do they like B2C ecommerce plays or B2B enterprise software deals or both? Don't worry too much about competing in some ways with another of their listed portfolio companies. Many VC will place multiple bets when they like a market sector often betting as much on the sector as on a specific company.

For example, if a VC made a fifty-X return in their last fund on one of their portfolio companies that was in the online publishing space then they are more likely to understand and like that space. To get an investment done with any VC you need a *champion* within that firm. Look over the biographies of each partner on the firm's website and see if there is someone who would really understand and be comfortable with what you are proposing. The other partners will look to this person for advice concerning your venture. If your idea and plan are solid, then the closer your champion's familiarity with what you are trying to do, the better your chances of winning him or her over and getting an investment. If you don't see anyone on the VC team with some background in what you are doing, then it is unlikely that you will find the required champion you need.

Another factor for your list is to know where a VC's fund is in its life cycle. When a VC firm first opens a new fund, they have a lot of money to invest and tend to be more aggressive in doing deals. VCs tend to get much more selective towards the end of their fund when they know that they can only do one or two more deals.

The size of the fund is also important. The fund managers only have so much time and it can cost them just as much time to do a small investment as to do a large one. Usually a $200M fund is not going to be deploying it in $250K rounds, but a $10M fund might.

Don't forget to include family funds. Wealthy individuals sometimes establish a small fund and have one of their kids (whichever one got an MBA) to run it. These funds are typically evergreen and often get less deal flow. I have found them less stringent with their criteria than a typical VC. Often, the patriarch's passions and interests are as big of a factor as financial returns to these groups.

There aren't many venture capitalists that do very early stage or pre-revenue round investing for a first time entrepreneur. For your initial capital, you are most likely going to need to approach angels. Angel investors and angels groups typically aren't professional fulltime investors like the VCs. Angels may be wealthy individuals or ex-entrepreneurs themselves who spend some of their time looking for local opportunities. They can be very sophisticated investors or occasionally not sophisticated at all. They focus on investing in very early stage ventures where the company valuations are low enough that their smaller size investments can still buy a good chunk of equity. They are not typically limited by a fund's investment criteria but they are very partial towards what they know and understand given their individual career experience. Angels typically don't require a proven business model. They are willing to assume more risk on unproven business plans in exchange for higher potential rewards.

Angel groups come in two primary flavors, those with a group fund and those without. I have been a member of several angel groups. They are all different. Those with a fund usually write bigger checks but may take a lot longer to do so. Some angel groups are led by a few VC-want-to-be's that will put entrepreneurs through a time consuming and hellish due diligence process. Most of these groups only meet once a month and even due diligence team members can have a hard time scheduling meetings around their day jobs. They sometimes lock entrepreneurs down from raising money elsewhere, via a no-shop clause in their terms sheet and then take months to complete due diligence. Even if the diligence committee does recommend an investment, a single member can criticize your idea right before the full membership vote and kill your deal!

This said, angel groups do fund deals and often have a member or two in the group with some specific industry knowledge and connections that can be helpful. In my experience as an entrepreneur, the angel groups without a shared fund seem to be more effective in that an entrepreneur needs to only sell one member in the group to actually raise some money. Even if some members of the group really hate your idea, they won't try to kill it publicly because they have no money in a shared fund that they feel they need to protect. These are really big generalizations I admit. Each angel groups is different depending on its size, member mix, and leadership.

When it comes to fundraising, just as it is with any sales process, it is best to get a *referral* if possible. Even if you know whom to contact, try to find an introduction through someone before knocking on the front door. Make as many contacts as you can on Linkedin® and ask the angels and advisors you meet for referrals. When you come through the generic door you are viewed as a sales person wanting something. However, if you come through a side door, there is a perceived serendipity in your arrival i.e. a unique opportunity that perhaps others don't know about or a deal that's not been shopped around.

You no longer need a written detailed business plan. Most investors prefer just a one to two-page executive summary, your slide deck, and your spreadsheet model. These can be reviewed quickly and represent the real meat of the opportunity, so don't waste time writing a thesis.

I encourage startup entrepreneurs today to model their businesses to not run out of money. This may sound obvious, but there have been times in the past (and I'm sure we will see them again) when many models were built to run out of money in favor of maximum growth until that point. Additional rounds of funding were anticipated and entrepreneurs wanted to maximize their valuations via the strongest top line growth possible. Those days are gone for now and it is far too risky to let your company run dry today. You may get the funding you need but most investors today will see that you are running out of options and take advantage of your situation by offering you fire-sale valuations. It will mean being more conservative and navigating slower controlled growth, but I encourage early stage companies to manage their ventures towards a cash flow positive state.

I'm not opposed to raising more money to grow faster when that makes sense, but I think this should be done from a position of strength and not desperation. Keep in mind that the success of your company and you personally holding on to some meaningful equity, are not necessary the same thing. I've had friends who founded and ultimately grew large successful companies, but because of cash flow issues and several rounds of funding at lower valuations than previous rounds (down-rounds), they had so little ownership left that they really felt no different than any other hired worker. I recently had one of my early-stage investments go public with a successful IPO, but because of several down rounds of equity dilution early on, I did not even get my original investment back! There are some venture capitalists affectionately referred to as *vulture* capitalists that specialize in finding distressed companies and releasing them of as much equity as possible. It's really tough when you find yourself running out of money and your back is up against the wall. Will you lay off a bunch of friends and critically important people or will you choose to accept money under onerous terms from people you really don't want to control your business? If you want to hold on to some meaningful equity while quickly growing your company, mind your cash flow and avoid those down rounds of funding.

The banker's hat is not just something you put on when you are starting your venture. Almost all ventures experience cash flow issues at some point, especially in the early stages. Both *slow* growth and *fast* growth can cause cash flow issues. The faster you grow, the more often you need money-to finance that growth rate.

Don't assume that working capital has to come from an investor. There are many ways to get working capital that do not involve diluting your equity. Customers and potential customers are often willing to fund R&D projects in exchange for special pricing or terms. Resellers are sometimes willing to purchase certain rights, such as territories or exclusivity to certain vertical markets for a time. The best way of all to generate capital is fast organic growth, which is achieved foremost by getting your product and sales model as accurate as quickly as possible. We'll discuss this more later.

Wearing your banker's hat well is more than just good financial planning. It's also about being creative. I met with an entrepreneur a few years ago and I was immediately struck by how tired and beaten he looked. His corporate training business had grown quickly, but then a sharp decline in the economy slowed his sales down dramatically, just as he had made some big investments in R&D and infrastructure. I could see the anguish and sleepless nights in his face. He was also carrying around the guilt of having to lay several people off who had recently left good jobs to come work with him. He was desperately looking for a way to keep his boat afloat and almost immediately offered to sell me equity well below its market value. I said, as an investor, that I'd be interested in that deal, but I've been an entrepreneur many times longer than I've been an investor. Most entrepreneurs can relate to the image of founders staring up at the ceiling in the middle of the night knowing that they are running out of air speed, altitude and options. I told this distressed entrepreneur that I'd consider his offer only if he first tried something first. I asked him to call his ten best customers and offer them a 5% discount if they prepaid for a year of his services in advance.

We met again two weeks later and as he entered the restaurant I was immediately impressed with his transformation. He was smiling and walked like a man with purpose; even a spring in his step. He told me that most of the companies he called agreed to take the discount and that in short order, his cash flow problem should be over. I missed out on a *vulture* capital deal but I made a lifelong friend who has now worked successfully with me on several other ventures. Remember that your best customers and even creditors are the last people on earth that want to see you run out of money. They will often work with you if you are up front with them and offer creative solutions.

Of all the various types of investors, *strategic* investors are by far my favorite. When you raise capital, a strategic investor is almost always preferred to a purely financial investor. Strategic investors are customers, integrators, resellers, suppliers, or other business partners that consider what you do to be a major benefit to their core business. They tend to offer better terms than a purely financial investor and bring much more to the table by way of advice, referrals, and other industry specific insights.

I started a software company once that enabled healthcare providers to share patient information in a more secure and efficient way. By far, the largest payer in my home state of North Carolina was Blue Cross and Blue Shield (BCBS). I was able to convince the management team that having a shared workflow with the major hospitals would reduce their administrative costs dramatically and that the providers did not trust the payers to be the keepers of that workflow process. As a neutral third party, my company could serve as the trusted information exchange that both providers and payers could accept. The BCBS team agreed and made an investment. More importantly, they gave my little startup the introductions and credibility it desperately needed to sign on every hospital in the state that following year. The BCBS CEO even joined my board and became a friend as well as mentor.

Many large companies today have a strategic investments fund. Unlike venture capitalists, their primary goal is not just to maximize their return, but rather to stay abreast of industry trends, emerging technologies, and markets. They want to make money but this is not their only goal They often view their investments as pet projects and spend a lot of time helping their entrepreneurs. The research, introductions, and credibility they afford can make your company and they tend to offer much better valuations than other types of investors. Strategics often becomes marquee beta customers that you may not have been able to get had they not first become an investor.

Anyone you are going to be selling to or buying from could be a cash flow partner. There are many clever ways to manage your cash flow that can dramatically reduce your need for startup and ongoing capital. You can approach financing from two directions; raise more investment capital or find a way to reduce your cash flow needs. Most entrepreneurs think only in terms of raising more capital and forget to think about approaching cash flow concerns from the other direction – reducing cash flow needs.

I was recently working with a bright young lady with degrees in textile engineering and fashion from NCSU. She had come up with a clever way to laser print on denim that enabled unlimited patterns and designs. Her samples looked amazing, but it appeared that she was going to need a lot of working capital to buy material in bulk, have it printed on, and then moved to a cut and sew factory. While running the numbers with her, I noticed that the majority of her manufacturing costs were going to the labor-intensive cut and sew vendor. I suggested that we take a road trip out to meet the factory owner.

The factory owner was clearly impressed with our samples. After spending some time touring the factory and getting to know the owner, I offered him 5% of our company in exchange for floating our receivables for sixty days. He agreed on the spot. Since we sold to retailers who paid us on NET thirty terms, this agreement was like having an extra million dollars in working capital! He also became a trusted advisor and partner. Had this pre-revenue entrepreneur raised a million dollars in starting capital at that time, she would have forfeited the majority of our equity and most likely not gained an industry insider advisor.

Most first-time entrepreneurs don't realize how important cash flow management is. Watch your forecast and act quickly to head off potential cash flow problems. Depending on your business, always plan to keep a few months of payroll in the checkbook for the unexpected problem or opportunity. Don't hesitate to cut deals that cause you to pay *more* if they enable you to pay *later*. In a startup, money *now* is vastly more valuable than money *later*. Rather than jumping right into fund raising mode every time your checkbook lacks a few digits, think out of the box and find clever ways to reduce your need for cash. You will almost always get a better deal, when managing cash flow, from a supplier, partner, reseller, or customer than you will from a financial investor.

Among their many uses, *stock options* are another great way to help mange cash flow. A stock option is the right to purchase company equity at a set low price or strike price. In a growing startup, these options can become very valuable as they *vest* (become exercisable) over an established time period. With limited funding, you are not going to be able to compete with larger companies when it comes to salary and benefits, but you can offer ownership to key players. Depending on the position and their track record for performance, these equity grants can range from .1% to 4% of your company. Making your key players owners in your business is a great way to motivate them and to manage cash flow.

Giving away chucks of equity via options may seem to contradict my "hold on to your equity" advice but stay with me here. Let's say you find the perfect person to lead your development or sales team. Maybe that person is making $180K per year in corporate America. You can offer him or her $90K in salary and a $100K worth of stock options. This almost always works out better for you than raising the additional $100K in cash from investors because the perceived value of the stock option can be subjective. I encourage key hires to take only enough salary to meet their basic living requirements and take the rest in options. I often tell them that no one ever got rich taking salary. It's all about the equity so let's swing for the fences together.

If startup cash flow management is all about money now vs. later, then stock options are a good tool. Unlike the equity you sell, a lot of the stock options you grant will never vest. Some hires will not stay for the full vesting period and others you will need to let go for performance reasons. Besides the productivity benefits of motivational ownership, if the company is growing, then the key hires will remain excited about their options and will most likely not push for as big of a salary increase in year two and three. I never regret giving out stock options because if the recipients don't earn them, they will be gone (fired). If they do earn them, then I am happy to see them get a big check when the company is sold.

Let's say you have done everything you can to minimize your cash flow needs but you still require equity financing to raise working capital. Once you have an interested investor, it's time to put on your negotiator's hat (which we will discuss in a later chapter). It is the interested investors' responsibility to present you with a term sheet, which is basically a high level outline of the terms by which they would be willing to invest. If you can't agree on high-level terms, then there's no reason to incur attorney fees to paper a final agreements. The most important terms include how much money they will invest and at what valuation. The valuation is how much they think your company or business plan is worth at the time of the investment. Don't be afraid to walk away from a deal if the terms are not reasonable. It is better to keep looking or even to walk away from your idea than to work yourself silly for years in a venture in which you have little or no equity after a few rounds of funding.

Investors will often present a "standard" terms sheet as if it's a take it or leave it deal. I assure you that all terms are negotiable and a good attorney will present you with a number of compromises with which to counter an offer. For example, if you can't agree on a valuation then perhaps you can agree on a sliding scale by which the valuation changes if certain revenue or other milestones are achieved by certain dates. If you achieve the milestone, then you have proven that the higher valuation was merited and if you don't, at least you know that the valuation being offered was reasonable. Be careful with this. We entrepreneurs tend to be very optimistic people! There are many such compromises and each can have positive and negative effects. Remember that although you are on opposite sides of the table now, your investor will ultimately become your partner in your venture, so try to ensure that everyone gets a reasonable deal and that you are fourth coming will all relevant information.

I could write an entire book just on the ramifications of the various terms and how they get negotiated, but until you are in the midst of actually doing a deal, this would probably just put you to sleep. For now, I'll just emphasize the importance of getting a good corporate law attorney who does a lot of early stage investment deals similar to yours and in your geography. Let your counsel guide you through the terms being offered, their ramifications, what's typical, and where you should push back.

I will make one terms-related suggestion here for first time entrepreneurs that many attorneys fail to fully appreciate. Try to keep control of your exit i.e. when you want to sell your company. Most successful ventures don't exit via a public offering (IPO); they get acquired. If you agree to terms that give an investor control over when or how you can exit your venture, then you are pretty much stuck working for that investor for as long as it takes. Your first exit can significantly change your lifestyle for the better and empower you to do another venture without outside funding. However, an early exit may not be what your investor(s) want. They might be willing to continue to roll the dice because they need to show a greater than five X return, whereas you might be very happy to walk away with a few million in your pocket.

There are some things you can do to improve your perceived valuation. Valuations go up as risk is diminished, so try to think of ways to make your venture appear less risky. Building even a simple prototype of your software or product can help. Mock up the user interface so investors can see how intuitive and real your idea is, even if there is nothing behind the presentation layer of your code. It makes it "real" for those who have trouble visualizing and it sounds less risky to say that you need funding to "finish" your software rather than to "begin" building your software.

If you can get a few letters of intent/interest (LOI) from potential customers, it will go a long ways towards showing the marketability of your offering. These are just simple non-binding statements on letterhead stating that a company is interested in buying, integrating with, or reselling your product once it is ready.

If you can attract some recognized subject matter experts or proven captains of industry on your board of directors or advisory board, they can also lend credibility to you idea. Offer them some stock options or better yet, try to get them to put a little money in on top of the options you give them for their board service. Investors will view their involvement as an endorsement and take comfort that those in the know aren't afraid to be associated with your idea.

Many factors can go into determining your company's valuation, such as the size of your market, market addressability, first mover advantage, competition, intellectual property, etc. You should have a working knowledge of what each of these represent and how it is calculated. Much has been written and is available on these topics, so I'll avoid reinventing the wheel.

I will say a word about patents because I see a lot of startups wasting time and money on pointless patent applications. Some businesses do require patents. For example, if you've invented a new type of computer chip or chemical compound, then go for some IP protection. Most startups don't need patented IP. It is particularly difficult to get a meaningful patent on application software. Even if you get a patent, you most likely won't have the financial muscle needed to defend your patent from poachers. In some situations, I've seen patents actually hurt the startup founders who in hindsight accomplished nothing more than to publish their trade secrets in a concise form for large competitors to replicate. Many investors will urge you to get patent protection because they think this demonstrates the value of the intellectual property and some patent attorneys always seem to suggest the same because, well, that's how they make money. You may or may not need a patent and it may help or hurt you, but one thing is for certain, it's going to cost you a lot of money, time, and mindshare. Don't just go for a patent unless it is going to provide real value.

When you present to potential investors, try to sound very focused on what you plan to accomplish. You may have all kinds of functionality you could add and other markets you could enter, but if you paint a picture that's too broad, investors will label you as dreamer who will chase everything and catch nothing. Successful entrepreneurs know that when resources are limited and you want to get to the moon, you have to put all of your gas into a single rocket. It is far better for one rocket to get into orbit, than to have five get almost there. If you do need to allude to a broader picture in order to show a large enough market, then make sure that you describe them as "phases," pointing out that you plan to focus like a laser on *phase one* before moving onto any future phases.

Remember to do background checks on any potential investor. Most entrepreneurs are so excited to get handed a check that they don't stop to ask, "Who am I getting into bed with here?" Believe it or not, there is a lot of money out there that you don't want. There are some investors who will give you $10K and think that you now work for them personally. Avoid people who might be investing money that they can't afford to lose and non-accredited investors who don't meet the minimum legal wealth standard definition. If things go badly, unaccredited investors have many more legal rights to claim that they were somehow tricked into investing or misled. There are a lot of mean people in this world who love drama and intrigue above all else, even financial return. God help you if you get attached at the hip to one of these sociopaths. Always run a background check on individual investors paying specific attention to the number of lawsuits with which they have been involved. If they have other investments, make sure you call up those founders for a direct reference.

Like most of my lessons, I learned this one the hard way. I took a small investment from a guy who ran his own medical business. A year and a half later, when my startup was doing well and his investment was worth many times over what he had paid, he stormed into my office saying that he was in the midst of a nasty divorce. He wanted me to write a letter to a judge saying that the company would not allow him to split his shares with his ex-wife. I said that the company had no policy like that and that it would be wrong for me to do such a thing. So he made up the story anyway and told the same in court. When I was subpoenaed, under oath, I had to contradict his story saying that I had said nothing like that to him. He was held in contempt by the court and so he sued me personally for one million dollars. He also sued the company and each of my board members.

My attorney said he was certain that we could win this case, but that it would be very time-consuming, take a few years, and cost up to $50,000 in legal fees. So, I held my noise and offered the plaintive $20,000 to drop the suit. He refused. Three years and almost exactly $50K in legal fees later, the final appeals ran out and all charges were thrown out. Even worse, while in the midst of all this, I found myself in due diligence with a Fortune 1000 acquirer for my company. The acquirer almost backed out of a lucrative exit for us because of this legal entanglement that they did not want to inherit. I was able to get the deal closed, but only by setting aside millions of dollars in an escrowed contingency fund until the matter was settled.

Had I taken a few minutes to check, I would have seen that this seemingly professional gentleman had been involved in nine other lawsuits. Vetting my potential investors since has worked well for me as I have not been involved in any lawsuits since, but I have seen some sad things. I've seen situations that required a unanimous vote of all investors where one mean bastard literally told all of the other investors that he would not sign off on the deal unless he personally got some preferred payout above everyone else. I've seen an investor try to cut off other sources of cash for his own portfolio company because he wanted to force it into bankruptcy and take it over. He actually called the company's strategic partner that was about to invest the funds needed and lied to that CEO saying he should not invest because the entrepreneur was not trust or credit worthy.

Mean and unethical people are like landmines. There are not too many of them, but if you engage one it is going to hurt. They can be investors, partners, and employees. Character matters so always try to ascertain the nature of people before you get too involved with them. Mean people give off clues to their nature if you pay attention. Watch how they treat the waiter who screws up their meal at a lunch meeting. Use some of the probing interviewing techniques discussed later in this book and if you get even a hint of a mean vibe, don't walk ...run the other way.

I love parables and fables that illustrate a life principle in a memorable way. You may recall the one about the snake who asked a duck for a ride to the other side of the river. The duck was obviously concerned, but the snake persuaded the duck by reasoning, "Why would I bite you when that would only cause both of us to drown?" Halfway across the river the snake could no longer help himself and bit the duck. As they both sank under the water the duck asked why to which the snake replied, "Well you knew I was a snake."

Unfortunately, our litigious system in the US makes it almost always worth someone's time to sue you without any merit at all. If you are in business it is not "if", but "when" you will be facing a legal entanglement. You will be accused of fraud, discrimination, sexual harassment and more by charlatans simply because they can. If you have a business, they figure that you must have some money that they can get. When they sue or threaten to sue you, do your best to pacify them or pay them off quickly no matter how much you have to hold your nose while doing it. Remember that bankers aren't emotional. They stay focused on the bottom line. They don't say things like, "It's the principle of the thing" because you can't take principle to the vault. You are going to get screwed sometimes just for being there. It's not fair because the world is not fair. The best you can do is to suck it up and minimize the distraction and cost as much as possible so that you and your team can get re-focus on the business as quickly as possible.

You may not naturally gravitate towards fund raising, accounting, or cash flow management, but these are important parts of your business. Remember that most failed ventures list "under capitalization" as the primary reason for their demise. It is often said that a well-funded mediocre idea has a better chance of success that an underfunded great idea. You don't have to be a banker or have a degree in finance, but you must be comfortable wearing the banker's hat to make your venture succeed.

The Construction Hat

OK! You've built a reasonable business model. You know how you are going to manage cash flow and you've managed to raise the necessary startup capital you'll need. Now, it's time to put on your construction hat and finish building that product. This chapter is geared more specifically to building a software product, but most of it is applicable to building any product that has various features and functions.

Even if you are a seasoned software developer, you may struggle with writing system specifications and product management, simply because these are very different skills from coding. Most software startup teams think that their product has to include much more functionality than it actually needs before they can start selling it. I encourage teams to avoid scope creep and get to a minimum 1.0 release as quickly as possible. It can be sold as a "beta" to set customer expectation. There is a catharsis in actually selling what you have and it most often leads to many great changes to design and prioritization that would not have happened had you not sold a minimalistic version first.

It is easy to spend a lot of money building in features and functionality that do not create significantly more value for your target market(s). There are some simple, but effective ways to ensure that you are spending your R&D dollars effectively. You need to constantly manage the value (sales benefit) of each proposed product feature against the cost (R&D time). Once again it's time to whip out your trusty spreadsheet and start building your product *roadmap.*

The first column header should be labeled "Feature". The second header should be "Value", then "Cost", and finally "Priority". List every proposed feature or functionality that you can think of on a separate line in the first column. This is just a brief few sentences to remember the gist of the concept. List every idea that anyone on your team has thought of or heard a customer mention. Research competitive product offerings and list competitor features if you think they are pertinent. This is the master feature list. It's best to use a shared spreadsheet that everyone on your team can assess and contribute to, including your advisors, with related industry subject matter expertise. Don't leave it to chance. Make sure everyone knows that the minute they think of something it should be captured and documented before it is forgotten.

To the right of each feature description is its sales and marketing "value". How much do customers want or need this feature? Is it critical or just a nice whistle or bell? Will they buy the product without this feature? Are there prospects who say they would buy your product if it had this feature? Do competitors offer this feature or capability and if so, do they tout it? The value scale can be whatever you think works best from assigning a letter value to using a drop down box of descriptive superlatives. When a feature is first listed, you may not know its value and this will have to be filled in later by speaking with your beta customers, industry advisors, and other research.

The final column is for "cost". Each feature needs an assigned best guess cost in development hours. If your CTO or team leader estimates that two developers could complete a certain feature in about two and half days, then the cost of that feature is five development days. I'll discuss the difference between the product manager role and the CTO/developer manager role in a moment, but for now it is important to note that whoever is responsible for managing your coders, is the person who should come up with these time estimates. This person will know his or her team and each member's strengths and weaknesses given a particular task. The estimate should be conservative and include the time necessary for quality assurance (QA) testing, data migration, modifications to hover and other help screens, training material changes if applicable, and basically everything required to push that code drop into production.

We've all heard that time is money. Nowhere is this truer than when you are wearing the construction hat. If you are not the person coming up with the estimates, you can do a lot of sweating under that hat. Time is precious and you will feel a huge sense of urgency each day as your pre-revenue working capital plummets. If you are not contributing as a coder, you will feel rather helpless waiting for the features you need in order to start producing revenue. It will be difficult, but I encourage you to always accept the estimates provided by your CTO without question. Never use those early estimates to criticize him or her or their development team. The features on the high level roadmap are not well defined and once they are defined in a specification document, the amount of time necessary to deliver them can vary dramatically.

Imaging being forced to estimate the cost of building a house from only a two to three sentence high-level description. Estimating software deliverables can be a very humbling exercise, even for a very experienced CTO or team leader. Sometimes an open source module can be located and implemented that knocks literally days off of an early estimate. Other times, coders can run into unforeseen complexities that bog them down for days.

Your CTO will not like giving you estimates based on a few sentences listed in the high level roadmap, but you must have at least a ball park cost estimate for each one. You should reassure your CTO that you understand how difficult this is and that you are not going to hold him or her to this best guess. This first estimate is just to help you or your product manager (who are probably one and the same) to decide which features should have a full system specification written.

Your features list may seem overwhelming, but it is important to capture this list and to keep it in mind as your development team architects your product. If they know that certain features might be added at a later date, they will often design the data model, interface and other parts of the system differently, in anticipation of having to support these features in the future. They may even stub in and comment where certain features connect once built. The more "heads up" you can give the development team, the better decisions they will be able to make and the less costly code refactoring you'll have to do in the future.

Once you have a first pass cost estimate on high level features, it's time to select which features will be in your 1.0 release and write detailed specifications for them. Some features are a must-have, while others should be selected on the basis of highest value (sales benefit) for the lowest cost (R&D time). If you feel that you need more time to research the sales value of a feature before prioritizing it, then finish the specs you can and get the developers started on those. Remember, you want the most minimalistic 1.0 release possible.

As a founder or co-founder of your startup, there is a good chance that you are the acting product manager. If you are going to wear this hat, it is important that you understand the gravity of this role. Your company will be no better than its flagship product. The product manager's job is to maintain the high level roadmap and to write detailed specifications for each feature before giving them to your CTO for development. If you are the CTO coding and leading the developers, then I would suggest that you avoid being the product manager. It is extremely rare to find a coder who can view product features and the user experience the way a non-coder can. Products designed by coders typically have a user interface that is a reflection of the backend procedure calls and architecture, rather than one that intuitively mirrors the business work flow and the way non-technical users would think the application should flow.

As product manager your job is to ensure that the product is as easy to sell as possible, as quickly as possible. You will constantly be prioritizing the high level roadmap based on new information. For example, your sales team might go to a tradeshow and find that a high number of prospects asked about a particular feature. Or, you may read in a trade journal that a certain report is likely to be mandated by the government or certification authority next year. A product manger is constantly searching for bits of information that can fill in the blanks and help to clarify how things should be prioritized. Good product managers are perpetually contacting customers and asking them what features they like best or least and what functionality they would most like to see included in the next release. They host focus groups and immerse themselves in the industry their product serves.

In the early days, the product manager is also the guardian of the user interface. Before a new release is pushed, product managers will often bring in groups of users to see if they can use the product as intended with little or no assistance. You'll need to watch intently at training classes and demonstrations to see where a new user's forehead crinkles in confusion. Wearing this hat means being fanatical about the user experience because, as your company grows, even a small non-obvious part of the interface can lead to thousands of frustrated customers and costly support calls.

Creating a good interface design and intuitive application flow is a combination of science and art as well as some trial and error. One of my startups involved using avatars for immersive online learning. Avatars had historically been associated almost exclusively with gaming, so a lot was riding on whether or not executives and professors would consider this modality a serious tool for business and learning. I intentionally brought in groups of older executives to measure their response using the platform. Unfortunately, they kept referring to their avatar as "it". This unsettled me because I just couldn't see mass adoption of anything considered an *"it"*. How could I get these users to relate to their avatar as their human proxy in virtual classrooms and labs? In response, I made a change to the account setup that allowed new users to personalize and select their own clothing for their avatar before entering a virtual classroom. I also integrated a technology that enabled users to upload a picture of their face, which was then mapped onto the face of their avatar. It was a subtle change in the next focus group, but it was enough to let me know I was going in the right direction. I had killed the "it" and everyone was now referring to their avatar as "me".

Unlike a written business plan, a written detailed product spec is imperative and one of the most time consuming and meticulous tasks you will face while wearing the construction hat. In many cases, as much time should be spent writing the product specification as is spent actually writing the code. The problem with developers is that they tend to give you what you ask for!

Every use case must be considered. Here are a few use cases to give you a feel for how meticulous developers have to be:

UC1:   User selects function one i.e. any function your product enables

UC2:   User selects function one but has not created an account yet

UC3:   User selects function one but has not completed a required prerequisite

UC4:   User selects function one but has not been granted administrative permissions for this function

UC5:   User selects function one but decides not to complete the process once begun

UC6:   User selects function one but loses internet connectively prior to completing the process

UC7:   User selects function one but then decides to also include X on the fly

You get the picture. Every use case has to be thought through in detail. What will you allow? What will you restrict? What various paths and error messages will you provide? The functions that will be performed most often should be the easiest to perform, the default, or built into the template. Any cases you do not document will be like an open hole in your application, waiting to trap and frustrate your users, or even worse, crash your application and corrupt your data.

The business uncertainties and the specifications must flow together in your design thinking. What if you decide later on that there is a better market for your product or that it should be dummied down to a web self-service purchase? Would the current architecture support that? Changes in specifications can take minutes to document, but changes in your future product can take many weeks or months to implement. This is because making changes to an already-released product requires supporting the release already in circulation, while also creating a new release and mapping current data to the new structure while the product is in use. Coders refer to this as changing the tires on the truck while going seventy miles per hour.

Developers should always have good written specification in front of them. Developers without clear written specifications and a target deadline, will often begin to develop their own functionality or tangential projects; such as rewriting a section of their code to see if they can achieve the same functionality using less lines of code or a more creative algorithm. Developers take pride in their work and if given too much time to polish, that last 5% can double the required R&D hours.

Features are prioritized on the high-level roadmap spreadsheet. In prioritizing features and releases, you have to weigh the sales and marketing benefits of each proposed feature on the roadmap against its R&D cost. It's not as simple as it sounds. Some features may logically have to be completed before others and there are tasks that will need to be done in support of product scalability and robustness that aren't even on your new feature list. Product management is the bridge between R&D and S&M (sales and marketing). You can't rearrange the roadmap every time a sales person hears about some feature a customer wants, even though most sales people really do think you should. Listen to your CTO when he or she tells you that time is needed for non-feature related coding. As your coders push to get new features shipped, they may not initially be able to include all of the scalability, security, and monitoring features that they would like. You have to make the hard decisions from time to time giving them some time to catch up and write important code that is not feature related. If you don't, then you're just building a house of cards that will eventually collapse and ruin your company's reputation.

If your product is even relatively complex, then you may need to include another column on your roadmap and in your decision-making called "risk". There are some new features that you can add to your product, like a new report that are very low risk and require little QA, but there are others that involve touching numerous parts of the system in diverse places. This significantly increases the likelihood of introducing bugs and therefore requires a longer and more thorough QA cycle. Honor the QA process. In your enthusiasm to get to revenue don't bully your technical team into saying what you want to hear. Early customers will tolerate the lack of functionality much better than a product that is not robust or intuitive. All software has bugs and if the bugs are numerous enough or severe enough, they can lead to serious customer and revenue losses. Risk is something that you *must* factor into your roadmap prioritization discussions.

It is always best to maintain a continuous dialogue with your CTO when it comes to product specifications and prioritization. Never just hand your written specification to your CTO. I always made a habit of asking my CTO to iterate back and forth with me on a spec. An experienced CTO will have good suggestions such as, "if you can live without this little part of your spec, then we can reduce the estimated development time by fifty percent." At this stage, the spec is a dialogue. The CTO needs to understand what parts of the spec are a "must have" and you need to know where potential time/cost savings might exist. Feature specs should go through a few revisions before being finalized and handed off to developers for coding. This will ensure that you are getting the most value for your R&D dollars.

After your initial product launch and as your customer base begins to grow, you will need to start maintaining another important continuous dialogue with the person doing or managing your support/help desk. It's everyone's job to find and report bugs, but your support manager will be most familiar with which bugs are causing your customers the most pain and frustration. With each new product version release, the most severe bugs should also have fixes prioritized along with the new features. These are tough judgment calls and lots of people will have strong opinions about this. Listen to everyone and then make the calls you see fit.

Managing a product from its initial release through the early updates and new releases, is where the real magic happens that will either make or break your fledgling startup. If your product is endowed with too many features, then you are paying too much for R&D and probably parting needlessly with equity to fund it. If the product is too light on high value functionality, then your sales team is going to struggle and your revenue numbers won't show the traction you need, thus leaving you once again parting with equity to raise more capital to get it right. In the early days in particular, it's all about product management and finding the right balance for each release.

As the CEO, your job is to trust, but verify. Your CTO should be enforcing a coding methodology that is efficient, extensible, scalable, robust, modular, and well documented. He or she should be doing code reviews periodically with developers to ensure a quality product. Along with many other duties, your CTO should be putting production-monitoring tools in place, as well as procedures to ensure automated warnings for quick recovery and maximum up time. If you don't have the background to evaluate your CTO, then you are going to need some insurance. I recommend having an advisor or firm do a periodic review of your company's code and processes. A competent and confident CTO should welcome the assistance and oversight. Make sure that you get a full report. Your company can survive almost any bad hire, but nothing will sink you faster than a CTO that launches you on a faulty foundation. Get an outside opinion from time to time and don't hesitate to demote or replace any member of your management team that is jeopardizing the venture.

On an important side note, I almost always push for an internal development team. When coders build a house that they know they will have to live in, support and build onto, they almost always do a better job and there is less loss of your core knowledge base over time. Offshore super cheap coders can have a strong appeal for a startup with limited funding. If you have the skills to write exceptional specs and closely manage an offshore team, then you might be able to make this work, but be careful. I've seen several startups meet their demise because of the failure of an offshore team to deliver.

As I mentioned earlier, it is important to try to get a minimalistic initial release to market as quickly as possible. You should have a good group of beta customers advising you as to what features are most important and why. *Beta* customers are eager early adopters, who, with proper expectation setting and careful listening, can become your greatest asset in building a solid product offering. They will also become your most loyal references. You probably ran into several of these while researching your idea. Everyone loves the startup honeymoon stage. This is the time before you deliver anything when everyone is excited about your pristine idea and potential. It's easy to win over beta customers if you position them as informal advisors. You want to build a product that solves a problem they understand all too well. You need their advice and in exchange for that, you will give their organization free or discounted pricing for a time. I usually start with free, but leave the door open to charge them a discounted or "most favored nation" price once the product is fully functional.

Positioning early beta customers this way is crucial and very doable. Everyone wants bragging rights that they helped design some software system that solved a real industry problem. They want to be able to say that they were an early part of a company that really took off and did great things. Since you are not asking for money, their approval process can be quick and simple. They are the best customers you will ever have because when they use your pre-released product and find all sorts of bugs and missing features, rather than being angry at you, they will feel good about it because they are just doing what a beta customer/advisor is supposed to do. When you are ready to ask for money, you will usually find them emotionally committed to the product because they helped to build and perfect it. You will have a built-in champion within these precious early accounts. When you are ready to launch your first non-beta release, you will already have great customer logos on your website and a page of solid references for new prospects to call.

Make sure you nurture these precious relationships throughout the beta process. Speak to them often and get their take on specifications and early user interface mockups. Be grateful and whatever you do, don't argue with them over anything. Some beta customers will want you to include functionality that is useful exclusively to their company and literally no one else. Obviously such features, if they even made it onto my roadmap, would be way down at the bottom of the list. I deal with these issues very respectfully, but explain that such features will have to be considered in a future release. Usually this is enough to side step the issue without losing one of your precious betas. Whatever idea they have, you assure them that it is a great idea and one you will add to the roadmap for full consideration at the appropriate time.

Remember to ask for things up front to set a beta customer's expectations. I use conditional logic because people are usually more willing to agree to a theoretical or contingent request. I phrase my *request* something like this, "If we do a good job and build a great product that really does meet your needs or solve this problem for your company, would you be willing to champion and try to implement this solution throughout your organization, serve as a reference, publish a case study with me, etc.?" This seems fair when presented this way. It is much easier to get beta customers to do things for you later on if you have already got them to conditionally agree to do so in advance.

Early stage product companies tend to push regular new releases. They have to in order to fix bugs and to make major missing features available, but over time the version release cycle should slow down dramatically. Each release or *push* to the web, requires a full QA testing cycle. If you are supporting multiple browsers, tablets and mobile platforms, each has to be tested again with each release. In many cases, every version of every browser has to be tested on every operating system. Before long, you have a very large spreadsheet of test cases that can require many days or even weeks to verify. So as the product grows, you will want to have fewer, but much larger version releases and try to minimize the inefficient QA cycles. Make the most quick release cycles in those early days because they will not last and you will not be able to innovate as quickly in the future.

The Marketer's Hat

Once you have your first beta release specifications completed and your coders are hammering away, you will have the time to try on your marketing hat and start building some of the sales and marketing collateral you are going to need. B2C sales are often all about the advertising, and instant gratification, but enterprise B2B marketing can be much more involved. Selling software to the enterprise is best achieved by positioning yourself as a valued consultant rather than an online retailer.

When I begin advising a new startup team, one of the very first things I do is help them develop and refine their master slide deck. Whether you are presenting in person, online, or via a pre-recorded video on your website, the master pitch deck is the core communication tool for your value propositions. We spend a lot of time on this deck because your website, sales collateral, marketing campaigns, sales scripts, etc. will all flow from this master message. Making this message crisp and clear takes several iterations. It is a function of who you are selling to and how you position your message against competitors. Word connotations, images, and speaking notes must be pitch perfect because mistakes made here will compound and flow to all of your other sales and marketing material.

The pitch deck should be able to stand alone or play a supporting role for a presenter. I like to type out word for word what I intend to say on each slide in the notes section. This enables the deck to stand on its own even if you don't get to accompany it. This is important because sometimes you don't get to present. A gatekeeper might tell you to just send your information over. Maybe the person you did pitch asks you to send follow up information which then gets forwarded to others who may not have heard your presentation. In a live presentation, attendees typically only remember about twenty percent of what you say. The deck with complete speaking notes serves to fill in the memory gaps. On occasions you may not get to present to the primary decision maker and you have to rely on the person you did pitch to, to forward your material. In this case, the quality of a self-sufficient deck and speaking notes on each slide can literally make or lose the sale for you. Another big advantage of having comprehensive speaking notes is for training. It is much easier for new sales team members to learn the corporate pitch if they have complete speaking notes to study.

Your sales deck is similar to your investor deck, except your investor deck includes sections not needed in the sales deck. Investors want to know things like the size of your addressable market, competitors, use of funds, and team biographies. Customers initially only want to know about the problem you are going to solve for them, how you solve it, and how much it will cost.

When it comes to pitch decks, *less* is usually more because the more you say, the less important each point will seem. So if you fill your deck with minor value propositions and superfluous stuff, it will only serve to dilute your core message. Discuss only one topic per slide. Use bullet points and tables to convey categories or lists. Don't use a font smaller than 20 points and don't include pictures or graphics unless they really do add to the specific point being made.

Your sales deck should start with your logo and tag line introduction slide. Here you state in a very concise sentence your mission statement i.e. the problem you solve and how you do it. One of my startups had this speaking note on our introduction slide:

"We lower corporate recruiting costs and improve candidate selection by empowering organizations to build a database of all qualified applicants from all sources and then share that information globally".

Another company I worked with had this opening statement:

"We make the healthcare data you need more accessible and less costly to collect by aggregating the data from major healthcare devices and phone apps into a single source."

Notice how each of these examples start with the benefit first (the why) and then follows with what they do (the how). We will discuss this more in the chapter on sales. Keep your opening overview very concise or you will get flooded with questions and may lose control of your presentation.

The next couple of slides usually discuss the problem and why the audience should care about this problem. Each slide needs a simple subject or title that clearly states the point the slide is making in one complete sentence. The facts stated below a slide's subject line, should only support the point that one slide title makes. It might sound like I'm belaboring the obvious, but you simply would not believe the unintelligible sales decks I wade through each day. Often the entrepreneurs are just too close to their solution. They lose the ability to think like a person hearing about their product for the first time.

The problem and (why you should care) section of the presentation is followed by slides stating how your solution overcomes the problem and creates benefits for your prospect. Depending on your offering, you might include a slide discussing how your solution is better than alternative solutions or typical ways the problem is currently addressed.

Your deck should also include a pricing slide and a credibility slide that includes customer logos and maybe a quote. Many enterprise solutions involve an implementation process. If it's applicable, discuss how you will migrate data, train staff, and ensure that your solution is fully adopted. Big implementations are scary and full of career risk for those who approve them, so be sure to convey confidence in your implementation process.

It's often advantageous to have an *appendix* to your pitch deck where you keep slides that you may or may not use depending on the prospect or what questions come up during your presentation. This is where I like to keep my competitor comparison grid. In my core presentation, I don't want to educate my prospects to competitive options that they might not know about. However, if competitors do come up in the discussion, I need a visual that will positively position my solutions against them. The appendix is also a great place to keep *objection* slides. These are common concerns or questions you sometimes get asked about when presenting. Again, you don't want to bring up concerns your prospect has not thought of, but if any do come up then you want to be armed and ready to address them.

A good example of an objection slide might be one containing some statistics from a recognized study that backs one of the claims you made in your main presentation. You need to keep your presentation down to a dozen slides or so if possible, so slides like this often get moved to the appendix and only used if you need them.

One of my startup's sold a platform for online learning. When presenting, I used to make the statement that most online learners do not watch an instructor's content. They typically prefer to open another window checking email or doing other tasks while just listening to the instructor's voice. Usually my audience at face value accepted this, but occasionally there would be an instructor or educator in the meeting who felt diminished by this and would in turn challenge me on it. I always kept the results from a large survey on a slide in my appendix section confirming this for such an occasion.

The competitor *comparison grid* is worth additional attention here. Besides being a part of your pitch deck, it can also exist as stand-alone content. The trick here is simple. If you get to select the comparison categories, then your product or solution should always come out on top. I am a strong believer in the second rule of marketing; "if you are not number one in a category then change the category". Products are usually listed down the grid with comparison topics across the top. If your product has certain features that are missing from most of your competitors, then these make for great categories. You can use checks and X marks to indicate if a feature or benefit is present or not. Often full or empty circles are used with a half filled circle when a feature is partially achieved. Your product should have all checks or shaded circles while all of your competitors should obviously be missing some. The visual message here is that only your solutions have all of these categories covered.

Besides the master pitch deck, there are other important pieces of collateral you will need. One important way to position yourself and your company as a valuable consultant and not a retailer, is to write a formal whitepaper discussing a best practice, key risk factors, etc. related to the industry or problem your solution is addressing. It has to at least appear to be objective and academic in tone, but there is a trick here as well. If your reader agrees with your logic, then you have won tremendous credibility and often a sale. If you position your paper well, then the only way the reader can implement that best practice or avoid those risk factors you discuss, is via the use of your solution. The "manifesto whitepaper" can be key to positioning yourself as a *thought leader* and your company as a valued consultancy. Your paper can be leveraged to get free speaking opportunities at conferences, interviews with influential analysts, and all sorts of other valuable press. It can be re-themed for different verticals and broken up into sections to support numerous marketing campaign content offers.

Surprisingly, it doesn't take very much research for you to know a lot more than most people know about their own industry, especially if you are selling to middle management. I believe it was Ross Perot, the colorful founder of EDS®, who estimated that if you read just one industry journal for thirty minutes each week, then you will know more about that industry than 90% of the people working in it.

I'm not sure why, but entrepreneurs are often reluctant to spend the time required to write a whitepaper even though they are typically only six to twelve pages long. Regardless of who writes it, it should always be attributed to you if you are the CEO or main company spokesperson. If you've done your research regarding your market and the problem you are solving, then this paper should not be too difficult to write. It's a great exercise to help you organize your thoughts and find supporting industry materials. The process of writing this paper is important because it will move you a long way down the path of presenting yourself as an industry insider and subject matter expert. This is always the position of authority from which you want to be selling enterprise solutions.

One of my startups was a healthcare communications company for which I published a whitepaper discussing the numerous communication dependencies that exist in healthcare workflows. I discussed a best practice of keeping all patient information requests in a common auditable and shared queue, rather than sending such requests to individuals. This approach reduced the potential number of failure points and enabled staff to work interchangeably. My "best practice" made a lot a sense to healthcare administrators and since my software was designed to enable just such a process, my whitepaper sold plenty of accounts without ever even mentioning my product by name. It also garnered me speaking opportunities at numerous healthcare administration conferences.

Keep in mind that your paper cannot sound like a sales pitch. It needs to stay focused on the problem, best practice, or risk factors stated in your title. If you do mention software that can address this problem or mitigate said risk factors, then you must do so generically wetting your readers' appetite, but never mentioning your brand by name or your paper will lose credibility. At the end of your paper, it is appropriate to have a brief paragraph titled,

"About the Author". This is your chance to mention where you work i.e. the name of your company or software. Some whitepapers also include a paragraph below this about your company. Make sure to include a contact for those interested in more information.

I want to make sure you get the tone of how these papers need to be positioned, so let's do one more example. One of my portfolio companies built a product designed to automatically archive the social media content belonging to government entities. I helped the CEO write a whitepaper on the risk factors associated with using social media. The paper pointed out that social media for government agencies, falls under the *freedom of information act* and as such, by law, it might have to be reproduced at anytime and at anyone's request. The paper discussed how difficult it is to keep track of social media two-way conversations that exist on multiple independent servers and it convincingly argued that archiving was the only sure solution for full legal compliance. Again, without ever discussing or selling his product, this CEO clearly brought attention to the need for a solution like his. He concluded with a nice "about the author" section and the business started flowing in from state, local, and federal agencies.

Case studies are another important part of your sales and marketing arsenal. Industry executives are always looking to their peers and competitors to see who is doing what. A case study is a brief (usually only three to seven pages) story describing a problem a company was facing and how they solved it. It must include some objective metrics showing a *baseline* before your solution was implemented and an improvement afterwards. It is fairly easy to get midlevel managers to agree to be the named author or co-author of such a study, especially if you write it for them and all they have to do is track the metrics. It makes them look good.

Keep in mind that you can only get a good case study if you have established a baseline metric *before* your solution is implemented. It's too late to ask for a case study after your product is installed and functioning. Managers will often need to get corporate permission for this, but if you can find a willing manager, it is better to just go ahead and write the study giving that manager the rights to edit and sign off on the case study as he or she sees fit once it's done. If it makes them look smart and the organization efficient, then it usually gets approved for public distribution. Jointly presenting a case study with an industry executive is the only way you as a vendor can get to present at some of the more influential conferences.

Campaigns that offer content are by far the most effective in B2B marketing. If you gate your content offer, you will be able to collect your prospects' company, position, and contact information. They will gladly trade this information for good content and if they are interested in your content, then they are probably potential buyers or at least influencers regarding the purchase of your solution. So, always be on the lookout for opportunities to acquire or create good content. Besides cutting up your whitepapers and case studies, you can also poll your current customers and publish the results as a "report". Comparisons make good content as well. Try to offer your content in an intriguing yet easy to digest format like "the four most common reasons why..." or "the five biggest pitfalls when..." Your content should always demonstrate a need for or point to the value of your type of solution.

I often advise, "It's easier to find hungry people than it is to try to make people hungry". Marketing is the art of finding those prospects most receptive to your message (ready to buy) and bringing them into a discussion with sales. Marketing dollars spent effectively can be transformational for a startup, but unfortunately, marketing can also be the black hole of precious startup resources. When entrepreneurs don't know what to do, they often simply throw more marketing dollars at a problem exacerbating the cash flow issue caused by a lack of sales. It can be a vicious downward cycle.

How can you spend your precious marketing dollar effectively? Before considering any marketing media, you first must build a *customer profile*. You don't have the money to go too broad, so you need to pick a single market segment on which to focus. When starting out, it is always better to look big in a small vertical than to go unnoticed in a massive one. Think deeply about who your decision makers are. What are their job titles? Who influences them? What do they read? What conferences do they attend? What thought leaders do they follow? How do they use social media?

Can you use a targeted mailing list to directly launch content offers to them?

Marketing spend is a function of how fast you can afford to grow and how addressable the market segment is that you have chosen. *Addressability* is the term used to describe how difficult/costly it is to generate the kind of leads you want. Until you are confident in your customer profile, be conservative with your marketing spend. Much of marketing is simply intelligent trial and error; so it's OK to make small mistakes, send up trial balloons, etc. so long as you can always track the results objectively. In the early days of marketing, I tell entrepreneurs that the first rule of effective marketing spend is "if you can't track it, don't do it." Startups don't have the resources for brand building campaigns, so every marketing dollar spent needs to be tracked back to the number of qualified leads and ultimately sales it generated.

I know that tracking marketing spend may sound obvious and trivial, but I guarantee that if you walk into ten startups today, the majority of them do not have a system in place for comprehensively tracking marketing spend through to actual sales. The second rule of effective marketing spend is to see rule number one... if you can't track it then don't do it. Once you find a media channel that is producing leads cost effectively on a small scale, then you can increase your spend. But you have to continuously watch the numbers. For example, LinkedIn® groups can initially provide very effective customer acquisition costs, but many of these groups are relatively small and dry up quickly. Just because something works for a while does not guarantee that it will continue to produce for you. Wearing the marketing hat means always looking at the numbers to make sure that you are getting a good return on your marketing investments.

There are many free and low-cost tools that can be used to track marketing campaigns and spending. There are email campaign tools that you can use to track open rates and perform subject line A-B testing, etc. Then, there are customer relationship management (CRM) tools used by your sales team to track prospects in the pipeline, schedule follow up contacts, and to forecast sales. The problem is that unless you purchase a fairly comprehensive S&M platform, none of these packages tend to work together seamlessly. So in effect, you may know that certain campaigns generated a lot of leads and you may know that you closed some sales, but you won't be able to easily track which sales came from which marketing campaigns or media spend. You have to connect the dots. Keep in mind that a campaign that generates a lot of leads from people who aren't buying is the worst possible result because not only did you waste marketing dollars, now it's killing the productivity of your sales team.

For years I used Salesforce.com®. It was affordable, included some nice campaign tracking capabilities, and many people I hired were already familiar with it. Today, Salesforce.com has become almost too expensive for most startups, but there are a lot of other CRM and marketing tools coming online. Whatever system(s) you choose make sure it enables you to track from marketing campaign through to a sale. I'll discuss CRM systems more in the chapter on sales management.

There are other software tools that you will want to have in your arsenal, such as those that do webinar automation. Webinars are another great way to offer valuable content to your prospective market. A webinar scheduled at a specific time can create the *sense of urgency* needed to move your to-do up on a prospect's priority list. Live webinars are great, but they can also be a big time commitment each week. There are very cool products now that enable you to record your webinar and then simulate a live event regularly. A good tool will enable you to even script the chat questions that appear to be coming from attendees. Simulated live events are convincing and I've seen them work well.

Remember to sign up for industry news feeds and set up ongoing web searches around key words related to the problem your solution addresses. I would always spend the first ten minutes or so of each morning doing this because it kept me up to speed on my market and it also provided me with lots of great marketing ideas. If you see an article discussing a law that might get passed or killed that would affect your industry, then think of how you could turn this information into a relevant and interesting webinar or content offer.

The tablet-based survey automation company I mentioned earlier came across an article that predicted that within the next few years there may be laws in the US, similar to those in Europe, that require restaurants to offer table-side credit card signing. This was a hot topic for restaurateurs and if passed, the law would mean that restaurants would have to make an investment in tablets anyway. If restaurateurs were going to have to purchase tablets either way, why not go ahead and get the benefits of using them now for survey automation? The team began campaigns with titles and subject lines like "How table-side signing will affect your business" and a webinar entitled, "The Silver Lining in Table-side signing".

Always be on the lookout for information that might be of interest to your market. If they come to you to get that information or commentary on it, then they will also get exposure to your product and solution. As with your whitepapers, these should always be presented as customer service announcements, factual in tone, and never come across as a sales pitch. However, make sure that somewhere in your talk or content that you work in a plug or two for your solution or at least solutions that do something very similar to what you offer.

Most early stage marketing is focused on new lead generation, but lead *nurturing* can be equally important over time. Lead *generation* is the process used to acquire new prospect contacts, whereas lead *nurturing* is the process of staying in touch with the contacts you already have so they don't forget about you when they are ready to purchase. B2C sales campaigns tend to provide instant gratification in that prospects tend to buy immediately, but B2B sales can have a long sales cycle. You don't often find enterprise prospects ready to change out their accounting system on a click through campaign! The B2B value seed needs time to germinate. Often, big purchases have to be approved for the following year's budget. Sometimes, prospects don't even realize the value of your solution until they have been educated on the problem repeatedly. And of course there are always those late adopters that know they need a solution like yours, but won't buy a thing until many of their competitors have already done so.

B2B prospects need nurturing. Find ways to regularly remind them that you are a valuable partner, subject matter expert, and solution provider. Offer them insights and relevant information that keep them coming to your site, reading your blog, and opening your emails without wanting to unsubscribe. If you are positioning yourself correctly and providing valuable information, then prospects will often forward your content or webinar invite to others, which will add to new lead generation. Keep pouring new leads in the top of your funnel while nurturing the leads already in the funnel and remember that good marketing doesn't have to be expensive; it just has to be good.

If your solution is targeting businesses, then you will probably find yourself at a few conferences and tradeshows each year. These can be critically important to your business, but expensive in both dollars and time so evaluate them carefully. I like to start out by researching and listing every possible show and event that would attract my customer profile. Yes, you need yet another spreadsheet! Add columns to show dates, costs, and other evaluation criteria. Here are some of the criteria I used to evaluate and estimate the potential value of conferences:

- How many people will attend the conference or show?
- How closely do these attendees match my buyer profile?
- How many of my competitors are attending?
- How many of my competitors that attended last year are attending again this year?
- Can I get a speaking spot or on a panel discussion?
- Will I get the attendee list after the event?
- How much of our time will this cost and what else could we be doing with that time?

Remember that speaking at any professional event is always better than being just a vendor at a booth. You have to stay well ahead of these conferences to get speaking spots. Speaker abstracts need to be submitted several months before an agenda is published. As with all marketing, track your leads and sales to determine whether an event or conference should be repeated.

To get the most out of a conference, you have to start setting up meetings well in advance of the show. Rebroadcast the event invitation to your prospect list and invite anyone planning on attending to come by your booth or to attend your speaking session. *Get on the phone.* Many of the prospects in your database will be at a major event or conference. Try to schedule as many meetings as you can. I've been known to have multiple breakfasts and several lunches on the same day! Set meetings up around breaks in the agenda and even host your own after-party. Facetime is precious and a gathering of qualified prospects can be an amazingly cost effective way to get tons of it if you do your homework well in advance of the event.

If you have a booth or table, make sure that it is always staffed. Make it clear to your staff that deserting their post is a serious offense. Train your booth team to always stand and make eye contact with each person passing by. Working a booth is not like other sales environments. In fact, the main goal should be *lead generation* not sales. The problem is that during a session break, hundreds of prospects may be walking by your booth or table. If you get sucked into a long conversation trying to sell one tire-kicker, a dozen other more qualified prospects will pass you by because you look busy or inaccessible. Some prospects plan to come back by later when you are less busy, but most get overwhelmed with everything going on and don't get around to returning. It is best to try to avoid long sales discussions during high traffic times.

Train your booth sales team to not engage prospects in pairs. Unengaged salespersons should physically distance themselves from the other conversation and continue making eye contact with each person passing by. The pitch needs to be short and concise. Once you have the prospect's information and a good short first impression completed, it's time to start moving that prospect out of your booth. Promise to follow up and do! If the prospect is very valuable, then suggest a later time when you can meet and discuss your prospect's needs in a less chaotic setting.

Events and conferences represent other opportunities as well. They can be a great place to make big announcements, roll out new releases, and to meet with current customers. They provide a wonderful opportunity to check out your competition. Stand inconspicuously in an adjacent booth and listen to their pitch. If a great prospect is speaking at an event, try to attend. When you email the speaker/prospect afterwards, mention how much you enjoyed the session and you will be much more likely to get a response. *Remember to walk around.* Shows are a good place to meet excellent, but unlikely integration partners and resellers. Remember to load up a bag of free marketing trinkets for your kids if you have any. They will think you're awesome when you return home with a bag full of flashy trinkets. If you want to know how valuable I think promotional trinkets are then just read the previous sentence one more time. Shows and conferences can be a big part of your budget so make sure you maximize their value by doing the things I've suggested.

A final responsibility of the one wearing the marketing hat is to be the sole keeper of the company's marketing message. Marketing is the developer, improver, and communicator of the "message". Sales people may carry the message, but it is marketing that decides what that message is and only marketing can make changes to the message. Don't let your staff create their own message. They can and should bring you ideas and suggestions, but marketing should always maintain tight control of anything being shown to the public that might affect the company's image.

The company's message has to stay consistent or it will get diluted and confusing. For example, you can't have one salesperson putting out stuff that says that your leadership development software is a *replacement* for traditional 360 reviews while another is saying that it is a *supplement* to the 360 review client's already have. It's likely your company message will change some in the early days and that's okay. Once you've settled on a message it's critical that your team communicates the message consistently. The most important thing marketing does for the startup is to keep the team using the same message and to make sure they know when and why that message is modified.

Is our offering the better, faster or cheaper option? What do we compare ourselves to and what comparisons do we avoid? Marketing makes these calls. Someone needs to be the chief marketing officer (CMO) and if you don't have someone who can sport this hat, then it is one you are going to have to wear.

The Salesman's Hat

A startup can survive and fix about any problem, but a lack of sales will end a new venture faster than any other adversity. As previously discussed, getting into selling early on is critical because it will enable you to test your message and value propositions while that early revenue can provide the runway you need to fix all of the other problems your venture will encounter. As an entrepreneur, you will be putting on your sales hat many times per day even before you start selling your product. You'll need it for fund raising, recruiting, managing, and more. Your ability to understand another person's perspective, effectively communicate your vision, its benefits, and deal with objections to ultimately bring others in line with your thinking is the skill that will make all of your hats fit better.

Some entrepreneurs, especially highly technical ones, shy away from wearing the sales hat.For them, the very word "salesman" conjures up images of an ethically challenged, fast-talking, information-withholding grease ball hovering around a used car lot. It's as if everyone assumes that a salesman's job is to get us to do something we don't want to do or to trick us in some way.

On the contrary, seasoned B2B sales executives are master communicators. They possess deep knowledge of the products and services they represent, industry standards, and competitive solutions. They are helpful consultants that take the time to learn their customer's unique needs and then demonstrate how their offering might meet current business and personal objectives. They ask probing questions and skillfully root out unspoken objections so they can be addressed. They would never lie or mislead a customer because they know that the trust and relationships they establish are critical to their reputation and future success.

The sales hat is honorable and critically important. The greatest discoveries of science would have wasted away in their labs had it not been for those dedicated messengers heralding a better way. Leaving no stone unturned, they are the most tenacious of all of the hat bearers. The sales hat is actually more like a helmet. Those who wear it have strong self-esteems that can endure dozens of rejections and dismissive insults each day without even taking a dent.

So what is selling? As a functional definition, I'd say that selling is the art of communicating facts and demonstrating how those facts relate to benefits that are important to your prospect. This may sound simple, but there really are a lot of ways to screw this up. Sometimes we start selling before we know what benefits are important to our prospect or why. Other times we lose credibility by stating opinions and then trying to present them as undisputed facts. Most often I see sales people firing off fact after fact, but forgetting to make the verbal connection as to why their customer should care i.e. how those facts enable various benefits.

Sometimes we are just selling to the wrong person or there are objections we have not yet discovered and disarmed.

The irony of selling is that it is profoundly simple and simply profound. It is a very simple concept, but because it is usually done extemporaneously while gathering information via a real-time dialogue, it requires you to be able to think on your feet, and modify your message as you go. This can make even a good communicator forget things and make critical mistakes.

Let's begin with a simple, but perfect sales combination executed by a table sales person.

This table is made of oak.

Oak is one of the most durable woods used in table making.

Durable wood is what makes tables like this last a very long time.

Notice how the sales person in the above combination begins by stating *facts*. When selling, you should always avoid stating *opinions*. A fact is an unarguable truth of which the vast majority of people would agree. A fact can be independently verified through research or proven by experts. Other facts this table sales person could have used might include:

1.   This table is not painted
2.   This table's joints are glued and double screwed
3.   This table is six feet long

4. This table was ranked in the top five in a Consumer Reports® review

5. This table has rounded corners.

Each of these facts can be proven and validated. They are not just personal opinions or subject to interpretation. The trouble with stating opinions is that if your prospect does not agree with them, then everything you said from that moment on becomes suspect. Your clients need to trust you. Sticking with the facts and never making an unsupported claim or stating a personal opinion is what gains that trust. It can be OK to state an opinion if the person you are quoting is recognized as an unbiased expert on the subject but all other stated opinions will get you into trouble. For example:

1. This table is one of the best on the market today
2. No other table will last you as long as this one will
3. This wood is really strong and durable
4. Tables aren't made like this anymore

These are all *opinions,* not *facts.* Sale representatives that start spouting off opinions lose credibility quickly with their prospects, but a well supported fact followed by a well connected benefits statement is the classic one-two punch combination in sales.

A *benefits statement* is the communication of a value for the customer made possible by a stated fact. Combined, this construct is a *facts/benefit statement.* It is the fundamental building block of all sales. Facts should always be followed by a clearly stated benefit for the prospect. The most common mistake made by those new to sales is that they tend to state facts about their product, but then simply assume that the prospective customer will make a connection to a meaningful benefit. This is a huge assumption and often very wrong. You must never fail to connect each fact you use to a benefit that the customer cares about.

Different customers have different buying motivations, goals, and problems they want to solve. For example, wooden tables do not rust. "Wooden" is the fact. "Rust-free" is one of the benefits. "Unpainted" is a fact that could be tied to the benefit of versatility i.e. the freedom to paint it any color desired. Double screwed and glued legs are facts that could be tied to greater longevity or less maintenance value propositions. "Rounded corners" could be tied to a value propositions such as *safer for small children.*

Start out by listing all of the facts you can about your product. Now start connecting the possible benefits each of these facts enables that might be important to your targeted customer. Once these are lined up, you can start to practice your facts/benefits statements. It is best to connect your fact to its benefit via a *bridge* or connector phrase such as "which means to you". Other connector phrases are "this is important to you because..." and "this really matters since..." The most important thing about using connectors is that they force you to state a value proposition.

Again, I know this sounds very trivial but I can tell you that not a week goes by that I'm not in a meeting being pitched by an entrepreneur or pitching with an entrepreneur that I don't hear facts being poured out without a connected stated benefit. Just last week an entrepreneur kept telling me that his product had connections to various social media. After which he would pause, smile, and look at me like a doctor who had just found a cure for cancer. The only problem was that I did not see the connection. I had no clue why his product needed to connect to social media or what benefit this fact made possible. Now I'm aggressive, so I asked for clarity, but many buyers will not. They especially won't if they are in a room full of peers and don't want to appear dumb or uninformed. I've made it a habit for many years to ask customers why they chose to buy or not to buy something. When they choose not to buy the reason given is usually, "I just didn't get it." Most often this is because the presenter did not make clear connections between facts and relevant benefit statements.

Wearing the sales hat means learning to think like your customer or at least to see things from a customer's perspective. Successful entrepreneurs eat, sleep, and breathe their product or service. They become so immersed in their facts, features, and buzz words that these become second nature to them and an intimate part of their vocabulary and thinking. Very quickly they lose the ability to think like a person who is being exposed to all of this for the first time. This is why the discipline of talking in terms of facts/benefit combinations is crucial. I've taken many sales training classes over the years and read books on most of the major sales methodologies. They all have their strengths and good techniques, but I assure you that remembering to speak in terms of facts and benefits alone as a beginner will get you further down the field than anything else.

It was reported last year that over half a million people who did not want quarter inch drill bits purchased quarter inch drill bits from Lowes®. Why? Because they wanted quarter inch *holes*! Remember that buyers don't want your software. They want what your software can do for them. You won't sell much software talking about your software, but you can sell a lot of your software if you focus on what it can do for your customers i.e. benefits. From cold call scripts to web pages, wearing the sales hat means learning to think and talk in terms of value propositions.

Sounds pretty simple so far, but here's where it gets a little tricky. All value propositions are not weighted the same by all prospects. If you go on and on about how your product has superior resell value and your prospect is never planning on reselling it, then you are going to come across as irrelevant and out of touch. *Talking* is the easy part of sales. The hard part is *listening*. Before you fire off all of those well-polished facts/benefits value propositions, you had better make sure that you targeted your missiles correctly. You achieve this by listening first to your perspective customer and by asking probing questions.

Back to the table example, "So why is it that you are looking for a wooden table?" Do you have small children? Will they be using the table? How often would you need to seat eight people? What did you like or not like about the table you are replacing? You don't have to sell a sophisticated product to be a sophisticated sales person. By asking these questions, you will not only be able to connect your facts to the right benefit statements, you will also start to gain the trust of your prospects who begin to see that you really are concerned about getting them what they need rather than just making your quota. The table example is simplistic. In the real world many factors come into play from budget to infrastructure to political considerations, but taking the time to really understand your customer's needs is how you will position yourself as a trusted consultant, rather than a manipulating salesman.

Keep in mind that a single fact can be used to support several different value propositions. Linking a fact to the wrong value proposition is not only unhelpful; it can also actually bring up new objections. I was once training a team of sales persons how to sell their instructor-led certified Oracle® training classes. At seven hundred pages, it was by far the most detailed and comprehensive Oracle courseware available at that time. During the live sales demonstrations, I encountered two very different types of prospects. One was concerned that the class would be too difficult and that it would cover too much material for him to keep up. To this prospect I used the facts/benefits statement on the following page:

Fact: *Our Oracle courseware has over seven hundred*
                 pages of material.

Connector: *This is important for beginners like you who are*
                 new to Oracle because...

Benefit: *You will be able to look up anything the instructor*
                 covered that you may not have fully understood
                 and review the concepts in detail with examples at
                 your own pace each evening after the class.

The second prospect had the exact opposite objection. He had been using Oracle for almost a year and felt that an introductory class would be too basic for his intermediate skill level. To this prospect I used the following facts/benefits statement.

Fact: *Our Oracle courseware has over seven hundred*
                 pages of material.

Connector: *This is important for self-taught engineers like you*
                 who may not have had a thorough systematic
                 introduction because

Benefit: *With that much material to cover, even an*
                 intermediate Oracle administrator is going to be
                 challenged and constantly presented with concepts
                 and techniques that are new.

Notice here how I used the same fact with both prospects but tied that fact to completely different value propositions based on their individual concerns. It would have been impossible to target these specific needs without first asking probing questions and taking the time to understand each prospect's specific needs. Firing off facts/benefits statements before listening to and understanding your client's needs and concerns is like a hunter shooting his gun into the darkness and hoping to hit something for dinner. He might succeed, but most often, he or she is just scaring away the game.

It can sometimes be difficult to get clients talking about what they need and why. I always try to have a few good probing questions ready to go. Here are some examples:

> *Why are you looking for a software product like ours?*
> *How are you currently doing this?*
> *What isn't working well with you current solution?*
> *Why is that important?*
> *What are your goals here?*
> *Which of those would you say is most important?*
> *And what did you like about that solution?*
> *Who else will be using this product?*
> *What are their concerns?*
> *What does that mean for you personally?*

A *dominant buying motivation* is the main thing a prospect wants to gain or the most important value they seek to achieve through a purchase. Although there is often one predominate pain point, there are usually multiple other buying motivations especially in

B2B software purchases. The art of sales is in identifying and uncovering all of these motivations and concerns.

Parroting is the technique of restating the buying motivations you think you heard back to your prospect. This is important for two reasons. The first is to make sure you got them right. "So what I hear you saying is...correct?" Remember that most people are not good communicators. I've repeated back word for word what prospects said to me before only to have them say, "No, that's not what I said"! Parroting is important because it helps you listen and it ensures that your prospects have communicated what they really meant. Once you have prospects acknowledging a list of goals, ask them to prioritize the list as to which motivations/goals are the most important and why.

The second reason for the discipline of parroting is that it communicates to your prospects that you are listening and care about what they said. You are also communicating that you really want to get it right and understand your client's needs. This technique is critical to establishing trust and a rapport with your prospect. Don't underestimate how important this is to the sales and relationship building process.

Whereas a buying motivation is what the prospects hopes to gain from a purchase, a buying *objection* is a concern, fear or any reason why a prospect may not want to commit to your product or solution. A seasoned sales person is an expert at rooting out all dominate buying motivations and objections. If you uncover and overcome every objection, then you will make a sale. Sales are most often lost because of undiscovered objections that are never spoken or rooted out. Again, probing questions are key such as *"what features do you need that aren't included in my product?"* or *"what do you like better about their (a competitor's) solution?"* It's the objections you don't know about that will most often cost you the sale.

Objection handling is also a bit of an art. It's very easy to work yourself into an adversarial role while dealing with an objection. Here's an example of a sale going south because of botched objection handling.

Client: *"Your product is more expensive than other solutions".*

Sale Person: *"No it's not."*

Client: *I know of at least two others that charge less for the same thing."*

Sale Person: *"You are mistaken."*

Client: *"..."*

Unfortunately, I've witnessed this particular calamity many times and it is like watching a train wreck in slow motion. It's been said that the only way to win an argument with a customer is to avoid it, but how do you tell a prospect or client that he or she is mistaken without starting an argument? Even if you prove that you are right, you will have most likely offended the prospect who now no longer wants to buy from you i.e. won the battle, but lost the war.

When a client challenges something you've said or you hear an objection in general, a flashing red alarm should go off in your heard as if a bomb has just been armed! If fact, it has and you must first disarm the bomb before you can proceed. When a client states an objection or contradicts a statement you have said, there is only one way to deal with it effectively and that is to disarm the bomb. Here's how you do it.

First, you have to agree with something the client said or at least affirm the client's right to feel or think that way. This disarms the bomb and gives you an opportunity to gently make your counter statement. This technique is best learned by example.

Client: *Your product is more expensive than other solutions". [Objection]*
Sale Person: *"It certainly can appear that way. [Agree/Disarm]*

Sale Person: *"In fact, a lot our my best customers said the exact same thing before they added up all of the extra modules they'd need to buy in order to get the same functionality included in our base product" [Counter]*

Another example:

The Startup Hats

Client: *"There's no way my team would do all of these steps". [Objection]*

Sale Person: *"Our best practice does appear to add more steps initially. [Agree/Disarm]*

Sale Person: *"That's why we include an extensive training program to ensure that your team realizes how a little extra work on the front end will save hours of extra work later on." [Counter]*

Other good disarming phrases that have served me well:

"I certainly understand how you might feel that way..."

"It does appear that way at first..."

"Some of my best customers have said the same thing before..."

"Yes, you are correct that in some cases..."

"There is an issue like that at first..."

"You are correct. That can be a problem. That's why we..."

You get the gist of this. A gracious disarming counter shows respect for your prospect's feelings and that you have the maturity and discipline to stay focused on your goal. You will discover that you tend to hear the same objections over and over again, so make sure that you create an objection-handling document with your best disarming responses and counters. Require your sales team to memorize this document and test each one of them via role playing. Involve your sales team in this process by asking them each week if they have heard any new objections that should be discussed and added to the document.

Remember that knowing the facts about your product and potential benefits is just the foundation of your sales process. You've still got to find the right decision maker(s), determine dominate buying motivations, ask probing questions, establish trust, and root out, disarm, and counter objections effectively.

There are several more advanced concepts that will sharpen your sales skills, but for now I'll just mention this one. Buying motivations can be either *organizational* or *personal*. Remember when you are selling that your decision makers are representing both their organization's goal and desires, as well as their own personal goals and desires. For example:

Organizations goal: *A better inventory system will help us work much more efficiently.*

Personal goal: *A better inventory system will get those guys in accounting off my back!*

Personal goal: *Less inventory problems means I might get home by 5:00 some days!*

Personal goal: *Fixing these inventory problems will get me noticed and maybe promoted!*

This is where the science and art of sales move into a grey area. Sometimes this is the elephant in the room that no one mentions. Corporate buyers don't want to admit that personal goals are part of their thinking and decision-making but they always are. If you can tactfully figure out personal goals and tie benefits statements to meeting them then you will be way ahead of the game. Anytime you can engage someone in both professional and personal conversation, you are well down the path of creating a lasting relationship. Probing questions of a more personal nature often work here to identify personal dominant buying motivations such as:

So this is a real problem for you personally?
It sounds like the current system is taking way too much of your time?
When that happens, does everyone blame you for it?
It seems like this could cause some pain points for you personally as well?

Establishing trust is also a critically important part of any large account sales process. Buyers are always in the process of asking themselves questions while you are talking. Is this sales person telling me the truth? Can this person deliver what has been promised once I'm committed beyond the point of no return? Implementing new enterprise software and changing established workflows is always a risk. Usually, a lot of time and money is at stake if things don't go smoothly and a really big batched install can cost an executive decision maker his or her job! Sales employees need to be sensitive to the fact these executives are always searching for clues to determine if you are trustworthy.

The main thing to remember when establishing trust is that little things don't just mean a lot; *they mean everything.* You are always communicating something. If you tell a prospect that you will send the proposal over tomorrow, but then you get busy and don't send it until the next day, then you are communicating that you may not be trustworthy. If you are even a few minutes late for an important meeting or forget to mention an additional small cost, then you are communicating that you may not be trust worthy. Most sales persons who lose a sale or even an entire account because of a lack of trust never even realize what they did wrong.

Establish trust through the little things. When a client asks you for something you should see it not as yet another inconvenient task on your busy to-do list, but as a precious opportunity to demonstrate trustworthiness. I even try to engineer opportunities to demonstrate my trustworthiness to prospects. For example, I'll sometimes commit to do something at a very precise time like 11:10 and then I will set an alarm so I can do it at exactly that moment. Look for ways to obligate yourself to a client so that you can demonstrate your dependability. I've had clients ask me for a certain document that I had in my notebook, but rather than just handing it over on the spot, I'd commit to send it to them as soon as I get back in my office. Once in a while, even if you know the answer to a client's question, tell the client that you will research that and let them know so that you can demonstrate that your word is your bond.

Don't forget the power of an *understatement*. If the client is really excited about your solution, it's a good time to do some *expectation setting*. Maybe point out some of the things that might cause delays or features that don't quite work the way they should yet. This may sound counter intuitive but you gain huge amounts of trust when you disclose minor flaws in your solution. When asked if my company would be there when needed I always took the opportunity to make it personal looking my client in the eye and saying that "*I*" would be there even giving them my cell and home numbers.

Many times I've asked customers why they chose to go with my little startup rather than a big competitor. Was it our better pricing or superior functionality? No. Most often the reply was something along the lines of, "I don't know...I just *felt* like you would honor your commitments and that we could trust you." They felt that way because I earned their trust through paying meticulous attention to the small things.

I think this should go without saying but always be *nice*. In your flurry of activity, stress and urgency, remember the human element. A startup is all consuming and a lot of stress can make you oblivious to the feelings of those around you. It takes a conscious effort to stay centered. Take a moment to learn something personal about your clients. A little small talk is important. People buy from people they like and they like people who seem interested in them. Being "all business" may be professional, but it is not *human* enough for most buyers. It is not our logic, but rather our humanity that connects us all and sparks that innate desire that most people have to want to help others.

In the early 1990's I was trying to start a company. It was an applicant tracking human resources platform that ran completely in a browser — something almost unheard of at the time. I was having a hard time getting venture capitalists excited about my technology because they had never heard of enterprise SaaS (software-as-a-Service) architecture. No matter how I explained the benefits and assured them that this model was going to become the norm, they just kept saying that they did not get it or, "Why do you want to *rent* your software." I did, however, find an angel investor who said that he would put in the $300K I needed to finish building the platform and launch the company, but only if I could bring him a letter of intent from a Fortune 500 company saying they'd buy it.

I had been pitching a large pharmaceutical company on the concept hoping to get a beta customer lined up for when the product was ready. With offices all over the world, my vision for this product was exactly what they needed but I knew that it was an incredibly long shot to get them to commit to an unfinished tool that they could not even try out. Reluctantly, they decided to form a committee to explore this new approach and make a recommendation. I was to meet the committee members for the first time on a Monday.

The Saturday before my first meeting with the committee, I had tickets to go to a large outdoor concert. I could only afford the cheap seats on the far side of the stadium, so I brought my binoculars. I was really looking forward to a couple of hours of relaxing downtime. Shortly after I sat down, a single mother with two small children sat down next to me without saying a word. As the concert began, the kids became really disruptive. They were upset that they could not see the stage and wanted everyone around to know it. I found myself getting angry because I just wanted to relax and hear the music, but rather than saying something rude I decided to let the kids take turns using my binoculars. Before long, the kids were sitting on my knee and having a good time describing everything they could see in detail. When the concert was over, the bedraggled mother spoke to me for the first time to say, what seemed to me, a heart-felt "thank you."

Stay with me here, I'm getting to the point!

Monday morning I put on my best suit and as I rode up the elevator to a conference room to meet the committee for the first time, I felt like a man who had picked a battle that he could not win. The door opened and there stood this same mother of two introducing herself to me as the chairperson for the committee established to evaluate applicant-tracking solutions! I'll never forget the surprise on my angel investor's face the following month when I slid a $500,000 letter of intent (for a product that did not yet exist) across the desk to him.

That company later sold for $100 million in cash. To this day, I wonder if that company would ever have gotten started had it not been for a simple act of kindness at an outdoor concert. I never forgot that lesson. If I had been in a bad mood, I might have really blown it that day. They say it's better to be lucky than talented. I don't believe in luck and I don't believe that nice guys always finish last, but I do know that helping the people around you creates an atmosphere where they want to help you if they can. My point is simply this: It doesn't cost you to be nice and it might amaze you how often those random blessings come around to bless you back.

I once helped a guy with a flat tire in a parking lot before going into a building for my presentation only to find that he was that company's CFO. I once let a contract employee out of his contract because of a personal issue. Years later he was in a position of authority at a big company I desperately needed as a beta customer and guess what, he returned the favor. In spite of my existential bias I can't help thinking that the Hindus may have the whole Karma thing right. It goes around and it comes around so never miss an opportunity to enact a kindness.

That's enough philosophy. Let's get back to sales techniques. The best techniques in the world won't be enough if you aren't selling to the right decision maker or if there are decision makers and influencers that you have not discovered. In a large account sales cycle, there can be, and most often are, several decision makers and those who influence the buying decision. For enterprise software purchases, decision makers fall into various categories. There's the technical decision maker, the business decision maker, and the financial decision maker, not to mention many influencers.

Each type of decision maker has his or her own criteria and primary buying motivations. *Business* decision makers generally want to know how effectively your solution is going to solve their business problem. How will it be implemented and adopted by staff? How will current work flows have to be modified? Will staff work faster, more accurately, and/or more efficiently? *Technical* decision makers usually have very different concerns. How difficult will this be to implement and support? How will data be migrated from current systems? Does this solution meet current security and scalable standards? Will systems need to be modified in support of this? *Financial* decision makers want overall corporate value. They want the best value for the lowest price. They are less concerned about a single department's business processes as they are about the overall company bottom line. What is the return on this investment? Will it generate saving through staff reduction? Will it free up working capital? Does it support a larger strategic vision?

The rule is "know your audience". A departmental business decision maker may not really care that your solution is less expensive than others on the market. His or her metric may be overall production/output. They may want the best possible solution regardless of costs. A technical decision maker may want the least invasive solution possible and could care less about features and functionality. Many times, you have to get a "yes" vote from each type of decision maker to win an account. A veto from any one of them can send you packing.

Sales fundamentals still work perfectly, even in a complex sales cycle. You just have to apply them in multiple places at once. First, make sure you know who all of the decision makers and influencers are. If there's a committee, then get all of their names and titles. Next, define each vote you need and what's important to each decision maker. Some have to be actively won over while others need only to be neutralized or pacified. You will also need to start mapping who the influencers are to each of your primary decision makers. An *influential end user* may have the ear of your business decision maker. End users may not give a flip about improved accounting accuracy or the cost of your system, but they may care a great deal about removing a particular aggravating or awkward function in the current system. They will have personal motivations as well. Find out what they really hate about the current system and show them how your solution addresses that. The lower the person's position in the organization, the more you should focus on personal buying objectives.

You have to figure out how to get all of the votes you need. Each pitch needs to be custom-made for that decision maker. The same fact/benefit that wins over one decision maker might get you a veto from another. For example, a financial decision maker might love the fact that your software will enable him to downsize twenty full time employees, but if you tell an influencer that employees in his/her department may get downsized, it's not going to be considered a benefit. They will probably come up with some other reason why your software solution won't work when they report to your business decision maker, but the real reason will be your failure to address a personal objection.

Being successful in sales is much more complicated than most people think, but it's not too difficult once you learn to think in terms of benefit statements. Ask probing questions and figure out what each person's buying motivations and objections are. Remember that once you have a yes vote, stop selling. If you keep talking you run the risk of creating an objection that otherwise would not exist. Take notes. Map out your large account strategy. Remember your sales fundamentals and you'll be fine no matter how long or complex your sales cycle may be.

The Recruiter's Hat

In my youth, I worked for a while at a staffing agency. It was just a placeholder job for me at the time and I had no idea how extremely valuable that experience was going to be for my career as an entrepreneur. This may be a hat you didn't expect to see in the entrepreneur's wardrobe, but I assure you that this is one of the most important chapters in this book. In fact, if your venture is very successful, you may even find that you are spending the majority of your day wearing this hat. As an entrepreneur, I was always amazed at how much time I spent each day finding, vetting, and hiring superstars who could do their particular job better than me. This is how you build a company beyond its humble beginnings. After your product launch and first revenue, as things really get going, you'll start to detect a subtle shift in your business. The emphasis starts to gravitate away from what you can do as a single individual and it moves towards what you can inspire and lead others to do. But before you can lead, you have to successfully recruit. Of all the entrepreneur's hats, this one is the least appreciated.

At one point early in my career, I had nearly two hundred software developers working for me at one of my companies. I had a reputation for paying my developers well, but that's not the whole story. When the company was just starting to take off I discovered something extremely important. As I assigned projects and reviewed deliverables over time, I discovered that the productivity of my few coding "superstars" was up to three or four times greater than that of my typical coder. It became apparent to me that paying my superstars a third more salary was a great value and no-brain-required decision.

The *superstar* phenomenon seems to hold true across all disciplines. It is a commonly heard statistic that in sales, eighty percent of a company's revenue is generated by only twenty percent of its sales team. A superstar is someone who has the full package. They have the drive, experience, intelligence, work ethic, attitude, and desire to really make a difference. A lot of their personal self-esteem is tied to how well they perform at their job and they are always on a mission. If you have a small startup and you've found even one or two superstars, then you are extremely fortunate.

Some of the largest and fastest growing companies today were built using superstar hiring policies. Managers are required to fire up to five percent of their lowest performing staff each year to create openings for potential new superstar hires. This may sound ruthless, but the logic is sound. Mediocre hires are the most common hires made, but tragically, they are also the worst possible hire you can make. Why? Because, you will fire a bad hire and get another chance at bat, but mediocre hires just hang around doing just enough; not really good enough to keep, but not bad enough to fire either. They are blocking the opening for that superstar that could be working for you.

Good recruiting is extremely important because more than your idea, business model, or technology, the success of your venture is dependent on the people you choose to hire. *They are the company.* Your venture will be no more exceptional than the people who comprise it. You are ultimately responsible for all of your company's successes and failures, regardless of which staff person did what. Whatever good they accomplish and whatever failures they cause, it is all on you because ultimately you hired them.

Almost all of the first-time entrepreneurs I work with struggle with the recruiting hat. Life in a startup is usually governed by "go as fast as you can", but when it comes to hiring, I encourage teams to slow down, take your time, interview several candidates meticulously, and make no hire rather than a mediocre one. As I've pointed out before, we entrepreneurs tend to be optimists. We expect things to go well and for new hires to just work out. In addition to this, we are always busier than a mosquito at a nudist camp. Sometime you may think that any warm body to carry some of the load would be better than what you are currently up against. Don't be lured into quick easy solutions. Most people aren't superstars and a good number of them can even make you regret ever starting your venture. Making a bad hire is always painful, but it is especially costly in a startup where founders are often doing most of the hiring and training. Your personal lost productivity is usually the greatest casualty of a poor hiring decision.

What would happen if your startup was made up entirely of superstars? Is that even possible? I believe that it is, but it requires a lot of work under the recruiter's hat and the stomach to let poor and mediocre hires go. Once you've got your product, pitch, and process down, it's all about the recruiting. The only way to increase the caliber of your hires is to increase the caliber of your hiring practices.

OK, I've probably beaten the importance of recruiting into your head enough. So how do you become a superstar recruiter? Recruiting effectively is a lot like sales, only harder because you not only have to find and vet the best candidates, you then have to sell them on why they should come work for your risky little startup. That sounds like a good outline for the rest of this chapter; 1) finding, 2) vetting and 3) hiring superstars.

When it comes to *finding* superstars, if you don't start recruiting until you need someone, then you are probably too late. Recruiting is something an entrepreneur is always doing. The way to get more sales through to the bottom of your pipeline is to start with more prospects in the top of your funnel. This same rule applies to recruiting. Successful entrepreneurs develop superstar radar. Everywhere we go, we are on the lookout for people who are at the top of their game; star performers in their current position. Superstars are rarely unemployed. They don't read the classifieds or job posts on Craig's List®. They are precious assets that have to be lured away from less satisfying situations, less lucrative positions and less appreciative employers.

It's time to add another tab to that spreadsheet called "possible superstars". Every time you meet someone who might be a superstar make sure to get contact information and to stay in touch. Send them company updates demonstrating what a great ground floor opportunity your startup is. Don't go for a quick close. Just plant the seed and keep watering it periodically. I would always try to keep a few dozen names on my list of potential superstars. They were my candidates in the wings and my first go-to list when a position on stage was created or came available. Recruiting takes effort and forethought. Attend entrepreneurial and professional events. Collect business cards from people who impress you. Write down the name of that exceptional waiter. If you find yourself talking to a group of sales people, ask them, "Who is the top sales person in your company?" Who's the best software engineer you've ever worked with; best marketer, bookkeeper, administrator, etc.?

I also maintain an email distribution list of people I know who tend to be in the know like attorneys, CPAs, accountants, bankers, professors, business journal reporters, angel investors, VC, and those guys who run startup incubators and accelerators. Whenever one of my companies is in the market for a superstar, the job description is sent out to my network. I always get a few potential candidates from someone who knows someone.

Although superstars are rarely unemployed, there are some exceptions. When companies go out-of-business, merge, get acquired, shut down an office, or announce a move out of the area, these are rare opportunities to troll for their superstars. Contact their out-placement office, post internal recruitment ads, and even consider running recruitment ads on local media following a big announcement.

A number of startups turn to staffing agencies, especially for technical hires where specific skills can be difficult to find. I've made a few good hires using agencies, but not many. Agencies add cost to your hiring and superstars don't tend to need an agency. Agencies can also be the bastion of short-term job hoppers who have a tendency to wear out their welcome in less than a year, perpetually needing a new gig. This said staffing agencies are sometimes a necessity while you build up your recruiting network. For short-term projects such as porting your code to another platform or device, an agency contract might be just the ticket. Agencies can also be used effectively if you negotiate a buyout option on your contractors enabling you to use agency staff as a candidate vetting pool. Still, the vast majority of your superstars are going to come from the network you build and nurture over time.

As with all prospecting, remember to always ask for a referral. If you contact someone who is not available or ready to jump ship, ask that person to refer you to someone else that they know and respect who might be interested in your position. Some of my best superstars were actually references for another candidate I was vetting.

If you are an entrepreneur, then you are always recruiting. I remember at one of my companies, that I sat aside a couple of hours every afternoon to build my recruiting network and candidate pool. Every week, I'd try to take at least one known superstar to lunch and just talk. I'd tell him or her about how much fun we were having at my company and how one day we would be working together. I knew that if I did not carve out and schedule that time on my calendar, then I'd get busy and always have an excuse to be doing something else. The first secret to hiring superstars is to recruit them before you need them. If you wait until you need a position filled to start recruiting, then the probability of making a knee jerk bad hire will go up exponentially. OK, you've built your recruiting network and have a decent pool of potential candidates. Now how do you know which ones are really superstars? This is where the science and psychology of predictive performance comes into play.

More than any other factor, the single best predictor of future performance is past performance. Spend a lot of time really digging into what a candidate did at each previous job. Resumes are generally evasive and inflated; so force your candidates to give you objective information. "So what percent of a typical day at that job did you spend actually coding?" "Of the ten sales executives there, where did you rank in terms of new revenue generated?" "Did you always make your quota?"

I've had to fire a number of employees that interviewed wonderfully. The problem was this. I simply was not skilled enough as an interviewer to create a clear picture of their past experience and attributes. Interviewing is hard work. Stay focused on your goals and don't let candidates off the hook until you feel that you have really gotten to an objective quantifiable answer. Some candidates, especially sales executives, can be very evasive. Here's an example of a skilled interviewer refusing to let a customer support candidate dodge a question.

Interviewer: So you worked as a customer support representative at that company?

Candidate: Oh yes, that was my responsibility.

Interviewer: Was that your only responsibility?

Candidate: Well I was a team player who did whatever I was asked to do.

Interviewer: So what other responsibilities did you have?

Candidate: I did some QA, management and administrative work as well?

Interviewer: So what percentage of a typical day were you actually on a support call?

Candidate: Well actually, I just took a call if the regular support guys were all busy.

Interviewer: Did you receive any customer support training?

Candidate: No, only the customer support team had to be trained.

There are other telling questions you should always include. Most established companies have some formal performance evaluation in place. This is a good historical place to drill down:

> *Tell me about your last employee evaluation?*
> *Did you agree with it?*
> *What were you praised most for?*
> *What areas for improvement were suggested?*
> *Do you think the reviewer was being fair?*
> *How did it compare to the previous assessment?*
> *Did you make any changes personally after the assessment?*

Besides having the particular skills and experience you are looking for, there are several other important attributes you will need to assess. A number of attributes have to line up to create a superstar; intelligence, experience, manageability, integrity, desire, creativity, work ethic, etc. A very smart and talented person won't contribute much unless they also have the drive to apply those skills. To use a car analogy, you need a big motor and you need some gas in the tank.

Until you get really good at interviewing, you may want to keep a list of telling questions in front of you as you interview. I like to organize my questions around the attribute that I'm attempting to assess. Let's start with manageability.

Manageability is the attribute that makes all of the other attributes useful. Back to our car analogy, a big motor and lots of gas aren't too useful if the steering wheel is missing! There are a lot of very talented people in this world with tragic authority complexes. They really struggle with the concept of being told what to do or having their performance evaluated. Rather than feeling pride that they accomplished an assigned task and contributed to their team, they will obsess over why that task was assigned to them in the first place. Was it worthy of my talents? Shouldn't other tasks have been assigned before this one? Will I get the credit I deserve for working on this? You get the picture.

Those with authority issues fancy themselves as managers, but because they have not yet learned how to follow faithfully, they will also suck as managers. Manageability issues at best create an inefficient drag on the company and at worst, they can turn into a cancer that can spread to others and undermine your authority. I'll discuss this more when we get to the leadership hat, but for now, it's sufficient to know that when you detect this personality trait when interviewing, you need to run away as fast as you can.

The good news is that manageability issues are relatively easy to spot during the interview process. Rebels just can't help, but to let themselves be lured into a discussion that in some way provides them with an opportunity to bash the object of their distain i.e. the guy unfortunately enough to have been their previous manager. I ask candidates who they reported to at a previous job followed by "tell me about that person's strengths and weaknesses." Keep drilling down with questions. If the candidate says the manager's weakness was poor communications or an inability to delegate then ask for some specific examples of times when the manager demonstrated this behavior. Don't let the candidate off the hook until you are completely satisfied. These examples are most likely burned in the candidate's memory." Surely you remember some instance that made you feel this way." Let the candidates talk. Those with authority complexes really are dying to tell you what an ass their previous manager was, but they're also trying to tell you what they think you want to hear. Keep giving them rope and they'll eventually trip themselves with it.

If you do have manageability concerns about a candidate, just keep drilling down on that attribute for as long as it takes. Another good line of questioning is to ask these candidates to tell you about a time when they believe that a manager acted immorally, dishonestly, or without integrity. Most candidates won't attribute these attributes to a manager, but those with an authority complex will jump right into personal integrity criticisms.

Obviously, there are some bad managers out there and people who unfortunately get stuck working for them. Don't throw out every candidate that's honest enough to tell you about an unpleasant experience, but do listen carefully to the examples provided by these candidates. Did the candidate act in a reasonable manner? Does he or she show any hints of compassion or empathy for the manager in question? Was there an unlikely pattern of bad managers?

Organization is another attribute you need to assess. Some people are real scatterbrains. They may have moments of brilliance, but if they aren't self-governed, it is unlikely that they will stay focused systematically long enough to make meaningful contributions. Dig in, "It sounds like you had a lot of responsibilities there...how did you keep up with all of that?" Ease into your line of questioning. You don't want the candidates to figure out what you are trying to assess and play you. Tell me about a time when you felt overwhelmed at that job and how you got control of the situation. Tell me about a system you created to help you organize and be more productive. You get the picture.

Keep in mind that even superstars are not perfect. A great candidate might still need some work on his or her organizational skills. The interview is not just about weeding people out. It's also about understanding what assistance your new hires might need and how best to manage them.

Drive is the fire-in-the-belly that engages the other attributes. There are some people, who have a "cruise to retirement" burnt-out mindset regardless of age. They want to do just enough to get by and to be liked by everyone. If you are hiring a receptionist, then this may not be as big of an issue, but if you are hiring a sales person, you'll need to really assess your candidate's desire to standout. "Where do you see yourself in five years?" What have you read/done/attended recently to improve yourself? Do they have ambition? What have they done recently to advance themselves that took effort? Tell me about something you did or achieved for which you are really proud. Here's a tip. Blank stares and cricket noises after that request should raise a big red flag!

Think about which attributes are most important for the position for which you are hiring and plan your interview around really digging into them. I like to separate the *skills* interview from the personal *attributes* interview. If you are hiring a coder, then make them take a certification test and/or give them a coding problem to solve on the spot. Have your best engineer grill them. If it's a sales person, they better be able to discuss the facts/benefits statements used in previous jobs and how they overcame common objections. Try to bait them into an argument to see how artfully they avoid the trap. No matter how well they do in the skills interview if they don't pass the attributes/character interview then they are not a superstar.

There are a few attributes that you just can't live without regardless of the position for which you are hiring. Manageability is one. Another must-have is the ability to be a team player.

Being a team player falls into the broader category of maturity. Emotionally immature people don't make good employees. They can create a lot of distracting drama in your organization. They are endlessly taking offense at something or someone and then launching an office campaign to see what other staff members they can get to agree with them on the matter. Non-productive water cooler talk goes up exponentially. Direct and efficient communication can start to give way to guarded statements navigating a minefield of petty hurt feelings. A small office can actually start to ride the emotional roller coaster of a single drama queen or king. If you sense possible emotional immaturity, then drill down into it with your questions. "Tell me about a time when a co-worker did something that was really upsetting to you." Fortunately, this is another attribute that is fairly easy to detect by asking probing questions.

Another byproduct of maturity is a reasonable self-esteem. I've known brilliant people whose great ideas often went unnoticed because of a lack of assertiveness. I'm much less concerned about a boisterous ego. True, they can be annoying, but if you're hiring superstars, then you are going to get some big egos. This type of energy can be channeled. Big egos respond well to goal setting, healthy competitions, and public praise. I've even found that an oversized ego is usually a telltale attribute of a superstar sales person. Low self-esteem is a real problem. It can be coached if you have the time, but in general, a startup needs assertive go-getters who will fearlessly go toe to toe with you and others in a room throwing out ideas, criticizing suggested approaches, and taking ownership of the risky process of uncertain decision-making.

We make a lot of mistakes in startups. That's how we learn. It's a good thing. Remember that you want to encourage your employees to make all of the mistakes they can as quickly as possible. Sounds silly but this is more of an attitude than anything else. If your team is not trying things in rapid succession and throwing out what does not work, then they are not learning what will work. Fast iteration is one of the primary strengths a startup has over big business. You want to foster that risk taking culture, so avoid hiring less assertive and less confident people who won't fit well into that culture.

Once you finished your interviews and think you may have found a superstar, it's time to start your due diligence. No matter how well a person interviews, never hire someone at face value. One of the best interviewees I ever hired turned out to have a serious drug problem. I keep repeating this because it's so important...past performance is the best indicator of future performance. There are some great actors in this world that can fool even the most skilled interviewer, but it is much harder to hide from your past.

I believe reference checking is as important as the interview process, if not more so. The only references you should check are those of managers to which your candidate directly reported. Don't bother with co-worker and customer references. You want to talk to the persons that were responsible for your candidate's performance. There can be a big difference between someone you like and someone who can be a great hire. One of my good friends that I've known and loved for many years would not last five days actually working for me. I know this because I did hire him and I did fire him. We still hang out. I know others who are absolutely no fun to hang out with, but who make exceptional hires. I may not go out drinking with them but in a real startup fight, there's no one I'd rather have by my side. Hiring is not about who you like. It's about whose performance you are going to like.

Don't delegate your reference check calls. They are too important and require skills similar to the ones you use while interviewing candidates. Managers, like most people, don't like to say negative things about others. Some are dealing with a little guilt for firing the employee and feel that they owe it to the person to help them get another job. You've got to dig down and keep asking questions until you are satisfied with the reference's responses.

Start out by confirming what the candidate told you as to dates, responsibilities, and percent of time doing various tasks, and then start digging into character attributes.

> *So would you hire this person again today to do that job?*
> *On a scale from one to ten, what overall performance score would you give this person?*
> *That's good. But tell me, why not a ten?*
> *In the last evaluation, in what areas did you suggest improvement could be made?*
> *Tell me about a time when this person exceeded / did not meet your expectations.*

Tell me about a time that you recall this person having a conflict with a co-worker.

You get the picture. The referral interview is very similar to the candidate interview. If you have concerns about an attribute from your candidate interview, then spend extra time digging into that attribute during the reference interview. As I said, hiring superstars takes time, but it is a mere fraction of the time required to hire, train, fire, and replace a poor choice.

Some managers, especially at very large companies, adhere to an HR policy of not providing references other than to confirm dates of employment. You can usually get around this using a little guilt trip psychology. First, confirm that your reference check and all information provided will be kept in complete confidence. Tell the manager that you cannot hire a candidate without his previous manager's recommendation interview. If managers insist that they are not allowed to provided additional information then say something like "Well, I'll let Mr. Smith know that he is not eligible for our position because you were unwilling to provide a reference." Pour it on if you have to, "You know, I received a reference call from your HR department regarding one of our previous employees just last month...don't you think it's rather hypocritical of them to ask for references on their candidates while not providing them to others? How do you feel about that policy?"

There is another big benefit to doing your own reference checking. I always ask the previous manager for advice, "If I'm going to be managing Mrs. Smith, what suggestions might you have for me?" How did you most effectively coach and get the best out of her?" Some managers will answer this question even if they refuse to respond to all others and the answers can be very enlightening. If you think you are leaning towards hiring a candidate then listen intently to what previous managers discovered worked well or not so well with that direct report. Some employees like a lot of hands-on involvement while others prefer more autonomy, etc. You'll learn which management style is most effective with a new hire in time, but a discussion like this with previous managers can really help you shortcut that process.

Once you've identified and vetted a superstar, how do you get him or her to work for your little startup? You are probably not going to be able to compete in terms of salary or benefits, but that's OK because there is something superstars want just as much; *relevance*. Superstars need to make a difference. Like all of us, but more so, superstars want to feel that their contribution is really important. Knowing that they moved the needle significantly and that they are greatly valued and appreciated can, at an emotional level, be even more important to them than maximizing their income.

Win your superstars over by letting them know that their contribution to your startup will be far more significant than what they can contribute to a larger company. You know how important they are and you need them. This may sound like a silly way to enter a compensation negotiation, but you're not going to win on dollars paid anyway. Look them in the eye and say, "Let's build this together. I need your advice and your experience." You've got to sell them on your business plan, your offering, and most of all, your unyielding passion to see it through.

Most superstars would much rather be a big fish in a little pond, than just another fish in a huge lake. They have often been affected by some really dumb policies and uninformed upper management decision making. Superstars love autonomy and efficiency. They hate it when things slow them down or get in their way. They really hate it when this happens and there is nothing they can do about it. When recruiting superstars, make sure you communicate that this is their chance to cut through all of that. They are going to have a seat at the table and be heard. You are going to listen to them and they are going to have the freedom to build, sell, manage, and/or set things up the way they see fit so long as they get the results you know they are capable of generating. This is intoxicating to real superstars who, like thoroughbred race horses, have been chomping at the bit most of their careers wanting to get turned loose and to really see what they can do on a wide open track.

Although cash is limited, you should have stock options that you can offer to help make up for lower salary and lesser benefits. Stock options communicate to superstars that you view them as partners. Stock options give them a degree of ownership and allow them to participate in the upside when their efforts help lead your company to a successful exit. I have had the privilege of handing out some half million dollar and greater checks to employees making less than $100K per year. It's a great feeling and when you start your next venture, those same team members will be ready to follow you anywhere.

Just as with any sales process, you need to be prepared to deal with objections when recruiting. Less overall compensation is one common objection you'll have to address. Besides offering stock options, I also like to let candidates know that if and when we are successful our compensation packages will increase proportionately. "Let's do well and be in a position to pay ourselves a lot more money." This indicates that you are aware that startup salaries are low and that it is your desire to see these improve as soon as the company can support the additional overhead.

Another common objection you will have to deal with when recruiting is the job security concern, especially from candidates that have family obligations. Most people have heard that startups are very risky and that most of them go out of business. An effective counter to this objection is to point out that big companies also tend to have layoffs from time to time, cancel new products and initiatives, outsource to other countries, go through mergers, and shut down regional offices which also cause unemployed workers. At least in a startup you have some control over the factors that would cause unemployment. I've had friends at the top of their game, with perfect performance reviews, who suddenly and unexpectedly received a pink slip out of the blue one day from their Fortune 1000 employer. No matter how hard you work or what you personally contribute, everyone working for a big company has this possibility hanging over them to some degree. In a startup, both good news and bad news are much more accessible. You tend to know what's coming down the pike and you get multiple opportunities at course correction. You have some control over your fate. You can often sell, build, or fund raise your way through the crisis. You will never be the surprised passive victim of a layoff notice because you will always have a fighting chance. Superstars love to hear this.

If you can't agree on a compensation package, then look for some type of merit-based compromise. "Yes, the company can pay that much if you can contribute X in new sales revenue or if you can get our beta product release shipped by a certain date, etc." You deserve and should be paid that much, so let's see what we'd have to achieve together to make that happen based on our model. In a startup we are all dependent on each other. We eat what we can kill and if you Mr. Superstar candidate can contribute as much as I think you can, then we should all be able to eat well before too long.

In closing this section out, there are some important exceptions to the normal hiring process that I should point out. Normally, it's best to build a network of good candidates, prequalify them, and keep them in reserve until you have an opening or your model tells you that you can afford another headcount. The one exception to this process is for the sales superstar. These rare birds aren't often available and they don't stay available for very long, so when you have the chance to hire one... just do it. I have never regretted making a position available opportunistically on such occasions. Sales superstars tend to pay for themselves in short order many times over. I am also much more generous with sales compensation. They will either be earning it or they will be gone because it is easy to measure how well they are doing.

As I think about all of my hiring mistakes and home runs over the years, I'm realizing that I could probably write a book just on hiring and training effectively, but there's enough in this chapter to get you moving down the right path. It's been said that you are what you eat. I hope not, but when it comes to your startup, your company is certainly who you hire.

The Manager's Hat

The manager's hat is the one hat that will enable you to take off all of the others to some degree. If entrepreneurs read and benefit from my little book here on how to put on the startup hats, then I would seriously consider writing another book called "Taking off the Startup Hats". It would focus on how to grow your venture beyond the startup phase by effectively learning to delegate those hats and responsibilities to others.

Successful entrepreneurs are typically movers and shakers by nature. We are almost always ambitious type-A personalities that move fast and get things done, but these beneficial traits early in a venture can turn to work against us when it comes to the seemingly slow and inefficient tasks of management, responsibility, delegation, and company culture building. What we can get by with in a small team can become a major problem as your venture grows, which unchecked can even be the primary cause of an otherwise excellent venture's failure. You pretty much have to be a control freak to successfully wear all of those startup hats required to get your company going, but you have to learn how to take them all off if you want to grow your company beyond what you as one individual can achieve. It's a bit of a paradox. The very personality traits that make you successful in the first place will cause you to fail just a short time later.

First time entrepreneurs view their company as their "baby" and as any parent will tell you, it is extremely difficult to learn to trust others with your baby. Founders tend to hold on to all decision making, rather than systematically preparing others and truly assigning those hats to them. A founder struggling with this transition will often tell a team member that from this point on you are in charge of something, but then never really give that new manager the authority needed to make decisions and act independently. Having created a team of impotent managers, founders can actually become their company's bottleneck, limiting continued growth because every decision still has to be brought back to them for approval.

Managers that have not been empowered are afraid to make decisions or to act decisively because they are unsure of what authority they have to make decisions versus what must be taken back to the founder to decide. At the same time, the founder, who once felt so efficient, is now drowning in a sea of details and has an even greater level of stress then when the company was just starting. Founders still trying to wear all of the hats can't keep up with all of the details required to make good decisions in a timely manner. Their decisions aren't timely and the teams implementing them don't take ownership of them because they feel that they had no say in helping to make those decisions. The frustration level reaches a breaking point followed by staff turnover. At this point, the venture either fails or the company's investors figure out a way to replace you as the CEO.

Unfortunately, I have seen this tragedy unfold several times. The problem is that that those startup hats keep growing bigger and bigger as your ventures grows. When they were little, you could work hard enough to wear them all, but as they got bigger, it became impossible to move under their weight and you feel as if you neck might snap at any moment.

The reason I'm qualified to speak on this subject is because I was once a really bad manager. I sold some of my companies way too early and left a ton of money on the table simply because I could not master the art of management and it was stressing me out. This is a very common problem for entrepreneurs. Of the dozens of startup technology companies that I grew up with that went public, I can think of very few where the founding CEO was actually able to make the transition from great entrepreneur to great manager. I've always had a tremendous respect for the late Steve Jobs who struggled so mightily with this transition that he actually quit the company he founded, but then returned years later with newly acquired management skills that enabled him to lead Apple® to unimaginable new heights.

As a fulltime investor and advisor now to early stage startup companies, I spend a lot of time talking to my CEO's and helping them with the various issues they are facing. I have found it far easier mentoring them in how to put the hats on then in how to take them off. The manager's hat is so different from all of the other hats. The other hats are about doing stuff quickly and efficiently and getting immediate results. Management is not a sprint, it's a marathon. If the other hats are about hunting, then the management hat is more akin to farming. It requires patience and I know very few entrepreneurs that I would call patient by nature. Being a great fighter pilot does not prepare you to sit in the control tower and direct all of the new fighter pilots. It is a skill that must be learned and it's critical if you want to continue to grow and remain in control of your venture.

One of the reasons the manager's hat is so difficult to wear is that it's not just a skill. It is also an attitude. Entrepreneurs like to tackle problems head on. Like John Paul Jones we cry, "Damn the torpedoes, full steam ahead!" We tend to jump headlong into a fight, start swinging, and figure it out as we go. Actually, that's not a bad approach to wearing a lot of the startup hats, except for the manager's hat. Transitioning to fulltime management means sacrificing what you alone can accomplish at the altar of empowering others. Entrepreneurs love to look back at the end of the day and say look what *I* did today. I built this or sold that. It's great for our ego to tally up a long list of wins throughout the day, but an effective manager is not afforded such immediate or direct satisfaction. Ours is the almost invisible hand directing others who lead their teams into battle and get credit for the victories. Our focus must transition from combat to directing our generals and the war at large.

Putting on the manager's hat is especially difficult because it's not a hat you can just put on all at once like the other hats. Ventures grow gradually over time. You can't just stop wearing the other hats one day and say you are now only going to wear your manager's hat. It is a slow transition that involves finding or recruiting team members who can wear a particular hat for you and transitioning that hat to them. It's not so difficult to think like a manager or a hands-on doer, but it's really tough to have to think both ways at the same time depending on the category or task at hand. As entrepreneurs, we get addicted to the individual successes we achieve each day. We see what we've accomplished and it feels good like a drug. Imagine how difficult it would be for an alcoholic if, rather than going cold turkey, he or she had to gradually reduce the number of drinks being consumed a little less each day over the course of a couple of years! That's what it's like to transition from the star doer to the manager.

OK, so we've talked about how important it is and how difficult of a transition it is so now, what is management and how do you do it? Management is the seemingly slow and inefficient process of defining and monitoring stewardships. A stewardship is a category of responsibilities for which someone has both the authority to select specific tactics and is held accountable for the results produced by those tactics. The foundation of good management is a well-defined stewardship.

Before I discuss the elements of a stewardship, I need to give you a warning. Never define your stewardships or write job descriptions in a vacuum. This should always be an iterative series of discussions that must include the person that will ultimately wear the hat being defined. I'll give you a bit of wisdom that I did not buy into at first, but one that I've come to believe is a timeless truism for any organization. ***People only support systems that they help to create***. I believe this to be the first rule of management that entrepreneurs must always keep in mind. Human nature doesn't change. No one wants to be a mindless cog in a machine. People don't want to feel used or utilized. We all like to view our self as creative and trustworthy to govern our own actions. Everyone knows that there has to be some rules that we will need to follow and that scarce resources must be shared. People also tend to understand the need to be held accountable for the outcome of their actions. These aren't the concepts that will cause your management sorrows. Get people involved in defining what their responsibilities and authority should be and how success should be measured? Jointly defined stewardships are the ones that people really take ownership of and they are immensely motivating.

Most first time mangers tend to screw up in the same way. They assign a stewardship, but then don't empower the person receiving the charge with the authority and freedom they need to pursue the objectives using their own tactics and techniques. The worst thing you can do to a subordinate is to try to hold them accountable for outcomes while dictating the tactics they must use. If they are not making the decisions, then you can't hold them accountable for their results. If you hold on to daily decision-making and dictate tactics, then it's not reasonable or fair for you to try to hold someone else accountable for the results. If you try, then you are setting yourself up to be called a dictator or micromanager and a mutiny is probably brewing. What makes a stewardship different from a job description is that it provides the person receiving the charge the freedom to pursue the defined goals their own way. This is not to say that you aren't available to answer questions, to discuss resource issues, or to bounce around possible solutions to problems. It does mean that once you have committed to release a stewardship to another person i.e. crowned them with a particular hat, then you no longer make tactical decisions related to that domain. Once a hat is handed off, you never put it back on your head, even temporarily, unless you are clearly and formally relieving that person of their charge.

Most people appreciate and find comfort in well-defined stewardships and a chain of command. When you ask someone to help you define a stewardship, you are communicating that you value their opinion and have confidence in their grasp of the goals and issues being addressed. If you jump back in from time to time and circumvent the authority you have promised them, then this will be interpreted as you no longer having that confidence or trust in their ability to make good decisions. You must *empower* your people to run their own teams or department doing things their way. This approach releases tremendous creative energy. If you make someone lord of a well-defined fiefdom, they will kill themselves to make you proud, but if you don't really honor their lordship, then they will never take ownership of their stewardship and they will resent you for the false title.

I think a maturing moment for me personally was when I realized that there are many viable paths to success. Just because someone does not do it the way I would does not mean that their approach is invalid or needs correction. In fact, you might even discover a better way. The bottom line is this. If a person accomplishes the goals you agreed to, do you really even care what paths were taken in the process? People are extremely fond of their own ideas. When you empower them to implement their own ideas they become profoundly committed to making those ideas prove out. This is the magic of an empowering management approach.

If you are new to management or to "good" management, then you are bound to make mistakes. You may have your life savings on the line, so when you think you see a mistake being made or know of a better way to proceed, the desire to grab that hat back can be overwhelming. Don't do it! It is almost always better to let a mistake go by then to tumble a stewardship. In fact, you want to create a culture where your people feel that it is OK to make mistakes. Stewardship owners need the freedom to try things and experiment without the fear that you are going to grab the reigns back at the first sign of trouble.

Sometimes the lord of a stewardship will try to shrug off some ownership back onto you, especially when outcomes seem uncertain. I've often had the owners of a stewardship come into my office and try to get me to make a key decision for them. Sadly, I used to fall for this one all the time. The minute you make that decision, you have released that stewardship owner from the responsibility of the outcome. You can suggest things they may want to try. You can brainstorm the merits of various tactics, but you must make it clear that the decision belongs to the lord of that fiefdom. You will not make it for them unless they are ready to forfeit their hat back to you. They alone are responsible for whatever happens, be it good or bad. The most motivating words a stewardship holder can ever hear from you are, "I have confidence in you and I know that you will do your best and that you won't let us down." Believe it or not, people thrive on that accountability and the faith you show in them is what will cause them to rise to any challenge. This is how you will be able to get the very best out of the people fortunate enough to work for you.

Honoring a stewardship also means a deep respect for the chain of command. Be careful to never assign tasks or give direction to someone that is not your direct report i.e. those reporting to a hat that you no longer own. This is difficult because when your team was small, the staff got used to coming directly to you for decisions when everyone reported directly to you. Now that the organization has grown, they have to learn another behavior pattern. Everyone prefers to go straight to the CEO or founder rather than going to their manager or team leader. If you let them, you are undermining their manager's authority and creating confusion in the ranks. What if their manger asked them to do something different? Every employee deserves to have one boss only. I know that it seems silly and inefficient when you know the correct answer not to just tell the person asking you what to do, but don't fall into that trap. It is disrespectful to your manager and it weakens the trust and stewardships upon which you are building your enterprise.

The first thing you should do when setting up a stewardship is to establish a definition of what success looks like. What is the goal you are aiming for? How will you know when you are on track? There are many ways to define success. Try to always state your goals in objective and measurable terms. Some goals are always present while others are shorter-term goals for a given week, month, or quarter. Following are some examples of goals that might be included in a stewardship.

> *Version 2.0 will be in beta testing before March 1st.*
>
> *We will have less than 2% customer turnover this year.*
>
> *Customer satisfaction surveys will average over 90% each quarter.*
>
> *We will be on the stage presenting at seven major industry conferences this year.*
>
> *There will be no severity-one bugs in our next release.*
>
> *All customer support calls will be returned within one business hour.*
>
> *We will sign up two major resellers in the second quarter.*
>
> *The average length of new contract terms will be two years.*
>
> *25% of new revenue will come from the financial market sector.*

You get the picture. Stewardships should have objective and clearly defined metrics that you discuss and negotiate with your stewardship owners. Never dictate these goals. Jointly defining a definition of success with a stewardship owner begins the buy-in process. The discussion should go like this. Here's what the company really needs and what I think might be possible...what do you think? What other goals should we be targeting? What changes should we be engineering our company and your team towards? Most people like reasonable challenges and they like having a say in what they are going to be held accountable for achieving. They also really like knowing how their part contributes to the company's overall objectives and success.

The other great thing about objective metrics is that you can tie compensation to them. Don't be afraid to throw in some BHAGs (big hairy audacious goals). These are stretch goals, but obtainable. Merit-based compensation such as a bonus or some extra stock options adds an extra incentive for extra hard work. They can also help to *gamify* a challenge making it more fun. Remember that rewards and recognition can be just as important as money. Giving plaques or a weekend away can go a long way, especially if they are accompanied by a public show of appreciation. Whereas merit based awards are earned and part of one's total compensation package, it's also great to throw in some *unexpected* rewards. Letting someone know that you know how hard they are working and that you appreciate them goes a long way. The amount of the award is not as important as the frequency and sincerity with which it is given.

Besides defining what success looks like, another important part of assigning a hat/stewardship is defining what resources the new hat wearer has to utilize. Everyone is competing for resources in a growing startup. Will I be allowed to utilize the admin person or graphic design person? For how many hours per week can I use them? Can I hire someone? Once we hit X goal then can I add another full time staff person or buy this software tool? If the lord of a fiefdom has to ask permission every time before he or she can do anything then they are little more than *gofers*. You know...go for this and go for that? A real executive is not going to work in a gofer role for very long.

Establishing budgets is a good way to empower your stewardship holders and to make them aware of the resources they can utilize. For example, an inside sales manager might want/need a new and more full-featured CRM system for tracking prospects. That same manager may also want to add another full time lead generation person and provide tablet PCs to all outside sales staff. Which do you approve? None of them because this is not your decision to make! (I really hope you didn't fall for that!) The empowered sales manager, lord of the fiefdom, owner of his stewardship, wearer of the hat accountable for all tactics and outcomes is the one who must decide.

If the sales manager comes to you asking for advice then you can and should give him your opinion. If the sales manager wants to beseech you for additional budget, then you can listen and make that decision because this would constitute a change to a stewardship, which is something that does fall under your senior management hat. How they utilize the resources provided to them must be 100% their decision.

A budget forces those with stewardships to think critically and to do resource balancing. They have to carefully weigh benefits and opportunity costs. A sales person working on commission will always insist that he or she can't do his job without more and more resources. They must have more leads to select from, more tradeshows to attend and more fancy material to hand out. They aren't concerned about the cost of these items or what other parts of the company will suffer if sales get everything they want. They think this way because they are hirelings that have not yet been given a stewardship with success metrics and a budget to control. Your stewardship holders must control their section of the budget or they won't make good decisions. It is this responsibility and the burden of the stewardship they carry, that transforms them from hirelings into the leaders upon which you depend.

Another thing that should be defined in a stewardship is limits on authority. A budget is one limit on spending authority, but there may be others. If there are certain things that you feel you need to maintain control over then write them into your stewardship agreement. Maybe you want to reserve a veto on staff additions or sign off authority on expenditure greater than a certain amount. These are OK so long as there are not too many of them, and they are negotiated and defined up front.

Defining a stewardship and officially handing off a hat to a subordinate is just the first step in managing. If your hat wearer is new to the job, he or she will need some training. You may need to do the job together for a while i.e. you wear the hat a bit longer while explaining the reasoning behind everything you are doing and why. Don't do what many entrepreneurs do i.e. slap a hat on some poor worker in a knee-jerking act of desperation when you finally decide you just can't take it anymore. Handing a hat off is a big deal. You want to make sure you select the right person to wear it and that you prepare that person for the load.

Making the transition from doer to enabler/supporter is difficult. It's scary to let go of that steering wheel. But even though you are no longer in that particular driver's seat, you can still look out the window for warning signs and observe the gages on the dashboard. New managers need help. They need a boss with which they can be honest. Asking a stewardship holder if there's anything they need help with is not taking your hat back. It is just being supportive. Try not to be too critical. Constantly reaffirm your trust in their abilities. You want to build their confidence or else they won't bring problems to you or discuss their mistakes openly. If never ceases to amaze me how people can transform themselves into the image of what you say that you see in them.

Keep an eye on the metrics. It has been said many times that managers don't get what they *expect* only what they can *inspect*. Inspection and full disclosure is your right and your responsibility per the stewardship accountability pact. If deliverables are missed or sales revenue slip, you have a right to ask why and for an explanation of the plan to get things back on track. They are called *direct reports* because they owe you a written or verbal report at least weekly. Make it clear that freedom and responsibility go hand in hand. This is the other benefit of a stewardship. If things really aren't going well, then the one wearing the hat knows that it is his or her fault alone.

Let an underperforming stewardship holder know that you will help anyway you can, but if improvements are not forthcoming then you will be taking your hat back. Don't make it personal. Let demoted team members know that you are sure that they did their best but that all people are not cut out for all roles. It can be as much your fault as theirs because you made the decision to put them into that position. If possible, work to find a role in your organization where that person can be successful. This is what good managers do.

Next to undermining the authority of your stewardship-holder the next worst thing you can do, as a manager is to ignore them. If you are someone's manager, then you owe it to them to meet at least weekly and even more often in smaller organizations. Don't just chat. Have an established format for your meeting that includes a review of the metrics, areas where assistance may be needed and top priorities for the coming month or quarter. I started keeping a shared online spreadsheet with each person I managed so we could see the top goals and re-prioritize them as needed. My reports and I would type in updates and questions into the shared spreadsheet so we'd always be "on the same page" and remember to discuss certain items in our next meeting.

Remember that if the stewardship you are handing off involves managing others, then you need to make sure that the one receiving your old hat understands everything that I've discussed in this chapter. If your company continues to grow and expand, then the process of making and mentoring your organizations leaders will increasingly consume your days. Finally, read everything you can find written by Stephen Covey on management. Although these concepts did not originate with him, he was the first master communicator talented enough to get them through my thick skull.

The Negotiator's Hat

I've never had a class in how to negotiate, but I think I've witnessed firsthand about every technique ever invented used by people sitting across the table from me. If you are going to be in business, you've got to learn how to wear the negotiator's hat. You'll have to recognize when others have it on and are using basic techniques on you. You can work yourself silly servicing a bad deal and it will still be a bad deal. Getting fair agreements in place upfront is critical no matter whether you are negotiating with investors, employees, vendors, business partners, or a potential acquirer.

Most people want to feel that they have pushed you about as far as you are willing to go before they stop negotiating. No one wants to leave the room feeling like they left money on the table. So the fundamental goal of good negotiating is to get the other side to believe that you have been pushed as far as you can possibly go.

There is an awkward moment at some point in most negotiations where each side waits for the other to throw down the first important number or key term. If you produce the first number then you run the risk of starting too high or too low as they may have started with an even more favorable number. If you wait for them to throw down first, then they may get an advantage of starting the negotiating closer to where they want to end up. If you throw down first and your number is too unreasonable, then you may offend them and kill any spirit of win-win that may have existed.

So, how do you start? If they throw out the first number you should always try to look a little shocked or at least surprised. If someone from your team is with you, make sure they know to play along. Wincing communicates that the number or terms suggested are far from your expectation. After seeing this, the people on the other side of the table may now fear that they have thrown down a number that you believe is unreasonable. They may also assume that they are now running a risk of killing the spirit of cooperation or even the entire deal. This puts them on the defensive as they now have to recover by demonstrating that they are flexible.

This may seem obvious, but if you decide to throw down the first number or terms, then it is always best to start out by asking for a lot more than you would be willing to accept. This leaves you room to compromise and enables the other side to feel that they have won concessions and done a good job negotiating the deal. Don't worry too much if they seem shocked or surprised. It's all part of the dance.

While negotiating terms, you should throw down some *decoys*. A decoy is a term or condition that you say you want, but really don't care that much about. Skilled negotiators always ask for something whenever they give up something. Decoys give you chips on the table that you can trade that don't really cost you anything in terms of where you really want to end up.

I was once negotiating with a team of M&A attorneys representing a Fortune 1000 company regarding the acquisition of my company. There were lots of terms on the table that I really wanted such as a larger cash component and guarantees that all of my staff would continue employment as part of the deal. I knew from researching some of their previous acquisitions that they liked to lock founders into a one to two-year earn out period. I wanted the vast majority of the payout upfront and I wanted to be able to immediately start another company I was thinking about. So, I threw down a decoy. I told them that I really wanted to have a three years employment agreement with a guaranteed big salary and a golden parachute should I be terminated for any reason. Ultimately, I was able to trade this decoy in exchange for a no-earn out of any kind.

Sometimes bigger companies and vendors will try to bully you using the power of *legitimacy*. They will hand you a preprinted agreement and tell you that this is what all of their customers or partners have to sign. It's the only "approved" form. Don't fall for it. I assure you that almost everything is negotiable. Hand it back to them and say, "So this means that you are unwilling to negotiate any of these terms?" If they are willing to negotiate as expected, then they will probably fumble or at least hesitate a little with their response. They don't want to say "no" when in fact they would negotiate. You have called their bluff.

You can also use the power of legitimacy to your advantage. Tell a potential reseller or partner that your terms are the same terms to which all of your other resellers agreed. This puts them in the position of feeling like they are being unreasonable by insisting on a better one-off deal. After all, none of the other partners felt the need to negotiate these standard terms. Hand your non-disclosure agreement to a new hire and state that it is the only one that has been "approved by your attorney and investors" i.e. there is no room for negotiations on this.

Don't get pressured into accepting any deal until you feel that you have had the time you need to really think through all of the terms and their ramifications. Take the time you need to talk to your staff and advisors about the opportunity and terms. Some negotiators will try to create an artificial *sense of urgency* to pressure you into making a decision and thus stop negotiating. I've heard it all. Our CEO is leaving town for a month and has to sign this deal before he leaves tomorrow. We are only going to go with whoever signs up first. This sale ends tomorrow. Prices are going up next month. Be assured that if it's a good deal for both parties today, then it will also be so tomorrow or next week once you have had the time you need to fully vet the terms.

Another technique you will often see is the "I'm not the person who is negotiating with you" positioning. The people I've encountered using this technique are some of the best negotiators I've ever seen. They cleverly position themselves as "just the messenger". They supposedly carry your terms back to their higher authority and then return with that person's objections and counter offer. They cleverly convince you that they are not the one you are negotiating with and that they don't really care about the deal. They then start to give you some suggestions on how you might get what you want from the real decision maker or what that person might be willing to go for. They gain your trust and before you know it they have moved around to your side of the table and are advising you on deal terms.

When I see someone trying to pull off this variation on *good cop-bad cop technique*, I generally just play along and let the person think that he or she has my complete trust. I may even comment on how much I appreciate the guidance. If you do this, your new advisor will assume that you are being completely straightforward because you have bought into the ruse. This puts you in a good position to use decoys or any of the techniques discussed in this chapter and have them accepted at face value. Just keep in mind that your new advisor is the real person you are negotiating with and you will do fine.

Remember that you, even as the CEO, can also use this technique. You may not have an immediate manager that you need to "appeal" to, but you probably do have a partner, co-founder or board of directors that you may need to get a consent from (wink, wink) before entering into certain deals or partnerships.

The Startup Hats

Even novice negotiators all seem to know the *split-the-difference* compromise. I want $600K and you want $400K, so let's split the difference and agree on $500K. Sounds reasonable, but that totally depends on where each negotiator started. When this compromise is offered, if you still aren't where you need to be, then try splitting the difference again. Watch carefully.

So you are now at $500K, but I really need $600K.
I could split that difference with you.
Let's go with $550K.

The "splitting the offered split" counter technique might be just what you need to make up the difference to make a deal palatable.

One technique I hate is what appears to be the *wear-you-down* strategy. This is when the other person just keeps coming back with the same offer over and over again stated in slightly different ways. They talk and talk and talk through endless meetings until finally you are willing to agree to about anything that will end the merry-go-round. This may sound simplistic, but it still get's used because it works.

Negotiators know that you are super busy and most likely still wearing many, if not most, of the startup hats. Your time is precious and every minute you spend on the merry-go-round is depriving your venture of its most precious asset. When your feel this technique is in play, get off the merry-go-round. Explain that the negotiations are taking much longer than expected and that you will need to send in an understudy or proxy. I have actually appointed my entry-level admin to negotiate on my behalf in these cases! I just gave her the terms I wanted and told her to keep negotiating until she got them. Negotiators find this really frustrating because basically you are now doing the same thing to them, but it's not wearing you down or hurting your productivity. It's usually not that long before they begin once again to negotiate in earnest.

A company just outside of Amsterdam once offered to acquire one of my startups. They offered to fly the partners over to their offices to negotiate the deal terms. After working a full day we flew all night and arrived at their office the next morning. As soon as we arrived they locked us in a room and we sat negotiating intensely for nine hours breaking only for one quick meal. They pushed us hard to make quick decisions concerning complex deal terms. We were young and inexperienced and did not perceive the various tactics being deployed. We were tired and just wanted some rest. We did OK on that deal, but I'm certain we could have done much better if we had insisted on some rest and taken our time. When you feel a full court press is being applied, back away from the table and insist on taking the time you need to negotiate a good deal with fresh eyes.

Remember that winning at all cost is not winning. Wars have been lost because of a won battle that ultimately was too costly. No matter how high the stakes may be, always be ready and willing to walk away. Every offer looks too good to pass up until the next offer comes along. I have a friend who argues that until you've walked away from the table at least twice, you are not really negotiating. I watched him do this at a car dealership. We walked out of the office and into the parking lot before the sales manager chased us down to accept my friend's offer. The *walk away* is a risky gamble because you might have your bluff called, but if the deal on the table sucks and it's not moving then you really don't have anything to lose. The walk-away has a powerful psychological effect. It makes the person left at the table feel that they have failed and having something removed from play always increases the desire for it.

One of the companies I invested in and advised had the good fortune to get a terms sheet from Mark Cuban, the famous investor from the popular TV series Shark Tank®. The terms were basically reasonable but Mark's attorneys were insisting on one term we could not accept. It, in effect, mandated that the company could not be sold without Mark's specific permission. I was concerned about this term because it could create a situation that put Mark and the two founders at odds. What these young entrepreneurs might consider a great exit might not be the same for a man worth $2.5 billion. The founders desperately wanted both Mark's investment and the credibility his involvement could provide, but with my encouragement, they had the guts to walk away from the deal. In this case, walking away worked. The shark blinked and called back offering to remove this condition from his investment terms.

One technique that has worked well for me and is less risky than the walk away is *the partial walk away*. It works like this. Rather than simply doing the *walk away*, you propose a lesser deal or relationship. This communicates that you believe the current negotiations are at an impasse, so you are giving up and moving on to another less difficult negotiation that maybe can get done. It might go like this. Since it doesn't look like we will be able to reach an agreement on an acquisition, let's discuss a possible partnership. Since it doesn't look like we are able to agree on reseller terms, let's focus on a possible referral agreement. Since I won't be able to meet your salary requirements, can we discuss a possible contractor arrangement? You get the picture. It convincingly communicates that you have gone as far as you can go and that you believe the other party has gone as far as they can go, so there's nothing left to do but punt. People often call a walk away bluff, but they rarely recognize the partial walk away as a walk away technique because you immediately start negotiating for a lesser deal. If the other party wants to get the primary deal done then this will put them on the defensive trying to get you back to the table. You'd be amazed at how often this technique gets the original deal done along the lines of your last offer before you executed the partial take away.

When negotiating, use your sales objection handling techniques to avoid falling into adversarial roles. Avoid flatly saying "no". Try to respond more with a "yes, if..." *Yes*, I could pay that royalty if you can agree to certain minimum revenue levels. *Yes*, I probably could agree to pay you that much if you can commit to this sales quota. As they say, there are many ways to skin a cat. Deal doing does not have to be black or white. Think in terms of "if" and "and"; a continuum; a sliding scale that triggers different valuations, exclusivity, or compensation level. There is almost always a way to get to "yes" if you think in terms of "yes, if..."

If you do happen to be pretty good at negotiating, allow me to give you some additional advice. Never negotiate a deal that is too one-sided in your favor. I used to do this occasionally because I could and I regret every single one of those deals. The only deals, partnerships, and relationships that work out are the ones that are good for both parties. The only partnerships that work out in the end are the ones in which both partners win. The only employees that stay with you and contribute for the long term are the ones with equitable deals and compensation. Just as there are some exceptionally sophisticated negotiators out there, there are also some very naïve ones that you can talk into about anything. Don't do it even if you have to do the negotiating for both sides of the table. You never want to feel like you took advantage of someone. You have a responsibility to your investors to make sure that your company gets a good deal, but you also have an obligation as a human being not to take advantage of others or to treat them unfairly in the name of fiduciary responsibility. If you plan on being in business for the long term, start building the personal reputation that you want to follow you. It is best to be known as a tough, but fair negotiator.

Remember that almost everything is negotiable. This includes the deals you cut with your vendors and professional services providers. You can blow a ton of money on top tier professional services if you aren't careful. Never just turn an attorney loose on a project without a set not-to-exceed budget. Ask your attorney to spend X hours on something and no more (depending on its relative importance) or you're likely to get a bill that burns your eyebrows off. What you'll get on a fixed price is often almost as good as what could have taken three times longer. Most attorneys have a bill rate that is several hundreds of dollars per hour. If you need a customer contract for example, try to find templates for what you need online and ask your attorney for a few templates for you to review. It is best to take a first pass at modifying documents like NDAs, privacy policies, offer letters, board consents, etc. yourself, and then just pay your attorney a set fee for reviewing your document. Once you are cash flowing, you can pay to have your documents reviewed again and upgraded. After all, who's going to sue a startup? You don't have any money! These documents typically aren't going to be what makes or breaks your startup in the early days. They should simply be viewed as administrative paperwork and moved aside as quickly and as cost effectively as possible.

In finishing out this section, I want to address a special negotiating situation I guarantee you will face early on in your startup.

Great sales people tend to be good at negotiating. They have leverage on you because of their revenue generation and they usually have a very healthy regard for their worth to your organization. If you don't keep this in check, then you can end up with another sales person in your office every week trying to renegotiate his or her compensation package. Sales people can be insatiable. In the early days you may only have one or two sales people generating most your company's top line. They see the company growing and suddenly realize that their sales contribution represents most of the company's total revenue. They can come to believe that their contribution is far more valuable than that of others on your team. These negotiations can be very frustrating.

It's important to keep your top sales people happy and motivated, but you also have to keep sales compensation inline. If you don't, then you won't be able to stay on plan or hire reasonably priced sales staff in the future. I make it very clear to my sales team from day one that I will only discuss compensation once a year. To do otherwise would not be fair to the other employees. I admit that sales are very important, but so is the rest of the staff contributing the other things. What if the developers argued for a raise every month because, after all, without them, we'd have nothing to sell? Make it clear that an employment agreement represents a one-year commitment. To try to renegotiate it part way through is not ethical. How would you feel if you weren't quite making quota and I suggested that we change your employment agreement to lower your base salary? Our model only works if sales costs stay within a set percentage of sales.

If you give in and renegotiate a comp plan mid-year, then you will seem unfair to your other workers who will now also be streaming into your office for consideration. You can certainly tell your top performers that you are aware of their contribution and that it will be weighed in mightily when it is time for the annual review and compensation discussion. You can also recognize top performers with unexpected rewards and recognition throughout the year, but never renegotiate a compensation plan midyear even if it means losing a good performer. Statistically, the vast majority of employees who only stay with a company in exchange for a midyear compensation increase are gone anyway within six months.

It is also important to know what not to negotiate. Very early stage companies, in my experience, tend to spend way too much time thinking about business development, partnerships and reseller channels. They view these as almost a silver bullet to scale their business. Although I've worked with some notable exceptions, usually very little value comes from these negotiations until your company has grown more organically. You generally only want partnerships with organizations that have a large sales force and customer base to bring to the table. Unless you have some key technology they strategically need, these companies rarely want to spend time talking to an early stage, unproven startup. But there are a lot of small companies and individuals who want to work with you at this stage. They want to meet and talk a lot and spent weeks negotiating revenue shares, complex contract terms, etc. They seem to think that you are their silver bullet! In my experience, 90% of these prove to be nothing more than a costly distraction. In the early days, your model and offering can and should be moving around some. Until you are experienced in selling your product yourself and have a set repeatable model, it is extremely hard to get others, who don't work directly for you, to do this well.

This said, you may come across some well-connected individuals that can and should be put on a referral agreement but these can be done quickly from a template document.

If a reseller model makes sense for your offering and you feel that both your product and sales model are mature then there will be a time for channel building and using all of the negotiating techniques discussed here. When you find yourself negotiating these relationships there is one additional important tip to keep in mind. If possible, negotiate for the right to directly compensate your partner's sales teams. Even large companies forget that whoever is controlling sales compensation is actually controlling the activities of the sales force in general. Sales professionals are most often coin-operated i.e. they follow the compensation. This makes sales compensation the rudder of the ship. If you negotiate for the right to provide additional direct compensation, bonuses, contests and other awards and recognitions to your partner's sales force then you will have some control over their behavior.

Another special negotiation you will have to face early on in your venture is negotiating with potential board members and advisors.

Like advisors, board members that are not founders or investors often work for stock options. Negotiating their compensation can be tricky because you have to estimate how much value and time each will contribute in the future. A lot of "advisors" go on and on about all of the contacts they have and how much they can do for you. But, on several occasions, after I gave some of these guys a nice chunk of options, very little of the value they promised was realized. Because of these experiences, I started negotiating with stock option grants that were awarded based on actual hours worked each month up to a maximum amount. In order to get their options, my advisors were required to send an email to me each month stating the hours they worked that month. Advisors were reluctant to put a large number of hours down because they knew that I'd ask what they did during that time. If advisors push back on compensation structured this way then explain to them that you like this approach because it makes sure that each advisor is compensated proportionate to their level of involvement.

Some entrepreneurs never get very comfortable under the negotiator's hat but it's one you must be able to put on from time to time. If you give everyone everything they want then your venture will almost certainly fail. Being a competent negotiator does not mean that you take advantage of people. It does mean that you have the skills you need to make sure that everyone in a transaction gets a fair deal or no deal at all.

The Sales Manager's Hat

Didn't we already talk about the sales hat and the manager's hat? Yes, but we didn't discuss the *sales manager's* hat. I believe this deserves its own section because getting your sales team going quickly is so important to your early survival. It is probably a hat that you are going to have to wear yourself for some time.

Whereas the sales manager role is a stewardship, your frontline sales reps will need direct hands-on management. Great sales people tend to be good communicators, tenacious and resourceful, but organized...not so much. They often shoot from the hip and chase anything that moves rather than implementing a disciplined process that ensures statistical success. Sales people, especially those new to the profession need structure. It's one of those catch-22 situations for a startup. You are most likely not going to be able to recruit a superstar sales manager until your company demonstrates some traction and you can't demonstrate traction without sales. So regardless of whether you have any sales management in your background, this is a hat you are going to have to wear for a while and a job that you are going to have to master very quickly.

The first thing you need to do is to arm your sales team with the tools they need to sell effectively. If you haven't given them the necessary weapons and armor, then it should not surprise you if they get slaughtered on the battlefield. I've discussed most of the sales tools your team will need in the marketing hat chapter. Just because *you* might have been good enough to close deals without some of these tools, doesn't mean that your sales team will. They need a master deck, competitive analysis, objections handling responses, scripts, case studies, white papers, and whatever other precious tools you can provide. These tools will increase their productivity dramatically like giving a ditch digger a shovel and a pick.

I was once asked to help a company decide which sales team members should be let go to create openings for better performing hires. It took me less than an hour to review the pitiful few tools and training they had been provided. My counsel was to keep all of the sales people, but fire the marketing and sales managers. It's just wrong to fire anyone until you have given them every opportunity to succeed and for sales people, this means ample collateral, training, leads, and management.

Unless your B2B sales are entirely self-service website transactions or through channel partners, you are going to need a well-trained direct sales team. After providing your team with the tools they need you then have to take the time to train them in how to use those tools. Have your reps present to you over and over again. Pepper them with objections, stopping to discuss each response and how it could be improved. When they've got it pitch perfect, let them listen in as you present to prospects. Only then do you let them present to prospects and this is done together as a team for a while.

My portfolio companies have told me that some of the most valuable assistance I gave early on to them was taking the time to listen to their sales people present to prospects and providing each of them with feedback. Feedback right after a sales person presents is extremely effective but this will be difficult for you to do. You will probably be desperate for sales and the urge to jump in to take over the presentation when it's not perfect will be overwhelming. However, do *not* give in to that impulse. Sit quietly and feverously take copious notes. A well-trained sales rep is the gift that will keep on giving. Training that rep through a live-fire exercise is far more important than making any one sale. Keep quiet and let the rep do the presenting.

It is impossible for a direct sales team to do their job without a CRM and it is impossible for you to effectively manage your sales team without one. The most difficult part of using Salesforce.com®, SugarCRM® are any other great CRM tool on the market, is not learning how to use the tool, but rather *enforcing* its proper use. Whoever is wearing the sales manager hat must occasionally get out a whip and make it perfectly clear to the sales team that using the company's CRM tool is not optional. Nothing but total adherence to its consistent use will be tolerated. Successful sales teams follow their sales CRM protocols religiously because this is the only way that they can keep up with the thousands of contracts, emails, and follow ups necessary to achieve quota. This is also the only way that sales management can get the metrics needed to understand the sales cycle, coach the sales team, and forecast revenue and cash flow needs accurately.

When it comes to managing a sales team, there is one important principle you have to keep in mind. You cannot manage a sales quota. You can only manage the activities that will most likely produce the desired quota. Sales activities are things like phone calls, emails, meetings, presentations, follow-ups, quotes, and reminders. The biggest obstacle to most sales professional's success is the lack of documentation discipline. They believe the big lie.

The big lie in sales is that some things are so important that there's no way you could ever forget to do them. I'm so excited after that great sales call that I'm sure I'll remember to follow up a week from now. There's no way I could forget that this decision maker is considering that competitor or has this objection or is influenced by that person. A successful sales rep is constantly in the midst of a flurry of activities with ever changing parameters. Weeks can go by before the next critically important activity is required. The busier sales reps get, the more they give into the lie. They justify the lie by reasoning that they are so busy right now that they don't have time to document that discussion or to schedule that follow up. I'll remember to schedule that follow up or send that document off tomorrow.

It never ceases to amazing me the important things I can totally forget to do when I'm super busy and under great stress, but there is a simple solution for total organization in sales using a CRM. Everyone who worked for me knew it well. I would start the mantra by say, "Do it immediately..." and they would finish in unison "...or schedule it". This is the golden rule of sales organization. There is no other way to maintain the required activity level in sales and keep it all under control.

Besides enforcing the proper use of the company CRM, one of the sales manager's key responsibilities is to help save sales reps from themselves. The way we achieve this is by establishing and tracking sales activity quotas. The right mix and volume of required sales activities is different for each unique business and sales cycle. If you believe that a new rep needs to make seventy phone calls per day to get three demos that will render one new customer sale, then establish these as activity quotas and build them into the written job description. Reviewing activity metrics is an important part of your one-on-one rep meetings each week.

Activity quotas help reps stay focused when the tasks that need to get done happen to be less enjoyable than other parts of their job description. Unless you are really into self-masochism, interrupting busy executives via cold calls is most likely not at the top of your list of most enjoyable activities. Humans tend to gravitate subconsciously towards the activities that they find more comfortable. In sales, this is referred to as *call reluctance*. Reps can come up with all kinds of "important" things that they need to be doing rather than making their sales calls. Presentations need polishing, bids need to be reread, and favorite friendly customers need to be chatted. These are all well and good, but often such things can simply be a form of call reluctance, providing reps with a subconscious excuse not to do the less enjoyable, but the necessary parts of their jobs. Having activity metrics is similar to setting goals or counting your repetitions when exercising. They keep us focused so we don't short change the less pleasant but important activities.

Another big part of sales success is in being able to show up at the right time. I always trained my reps to listen for clues when scheduling follow-ups. If you hear, "We will start working on our new budget in the Fall" and if the purchase of your product has to be budgeted, then early Fall would be an excellent time to schedule a follow up. The clues are abounding. Bill will be back in the office in two weeks. I can't consider anything new until I finish my current project next month. The new IT director starts in April. If you don't hear a clue and you know you've got the right decision maker, then just ask, "When would be an appropriate time for me to follow up with you." A lot of what a sales rep does is determine when to follow up with a prospective customer. If you are making hundreds of contacts a week, this is impossible to manage without a CRM. If you've identified some whales (decision makers who could make a very large purchase) and they don't call you back or respond to your emails, you will still want to remember to schedule touch points from time to time to remind you to send over a helpful article or webinar invite.

Over time as reps listen to prospects and schedule follow-ups accordingly, you will notice that their follow up call to sales ratio goes way up. This is because they are calling back more often at just the right moment. I used to ask my reps if they'd like to have a magic crystal ball that would tell them each morning which prospects were ready to buy. I'd let them fanaticize about how awesome that would be and then I'd tell them how to build a very similar instrument.

Beyond a simple scheduler, a good CRM will also help your reps manage their time most efficiently. Find a CRM that enables you to schedule both *timed* and *untimed* (timeless) events/activities. Untimed events/tasks are activities with a *date,* but no *time* associated with it. It is also important to make sure that the CRM you choose supports the automatic rolling forward of untimed activities to the next day if they are not cleared. This feature is a must for time management when selling. Stay with me on this and I'll explain why.

A sales rep's day is full of activities, which are either timed or untimed. Timed events are things that must be done at a specific time, like an internal meeting or a demo scheduled with a customer for 2:00 pm. Untimed events are things like cold calls and follow ups that don't have to be done at an exact time or even on a specific day. If you need to follow up with a prospect in the Spring, for example, then it probably doesn't matter if you do it at 9:00 am or 3:00 pm or even on the first or third of the month. In fact, you could probably do it anytime over a two-week period.

Sales reps need a CRM that enables them to schedule both timed and untimed activities. This really simplifies time management for your reps who now simply have to do the timed activities when scheduled and chip away at the untimed events in between. The untimed activities that you don't get to today automatically roll over to tomorrow.

I know this sounds ridiculously simple and obvious, but as Einstein once said, "Everything appears obvious once you think of it." You'd be amazed at the number of expensive CRMs available today that don't even support untimed activities.

A good sales rep very quickly generates hundreds and even thousands of untimed follow up events/tasks. It is *impossible* to manage these without a CRM that makes this distinction. I often point out that in sales all we really have is our time and how we choose to use it. Your best rep and your worst rep have the same number of hours to work each day. The only difference between them is how each chooses to use those hours.

The reports you get out of your CRM, if you know how to interpret them, can also give you precious insights into how to better manage and coach your reps. For example, if you see a rep with a high activity volume, but a low sales volume, then this usually indicates a *training* rather than an *effort* issue. These reps are working hard and getting in front of a lot of prospects, but not making sales so either they are selling to the wrong prospects are just not selling well in general. If you see a rep with a low activity volume, but a high sales volume then you probably have an *order taker*. Consider splitting his or her territory or handing off some house accounts and leads to the newer reps.

I always keep an eye on how many untimed calls each of my reps had rolling forward on average. If you don't see any untimed activities rolling forward, then either the rep is extremely new, not working hard, or has not yet grasped the concepts from your time management training. If the majority of your reps have good sales volume and lots of untimed activities rolling forward for extended periods of time, then it's probably time for you to increase the size of your sales force.

A common practice today is to promote your best sales rep to sales manager. This generally does not end well because, although some skills overlap, sales management requires a lot more skills then selling. In the recruiting chapter I referenced the sales 80/20 rule or norm, which states that in most companies, on average about eighty percent of the sales revenue is generated by only twenty percent of their sales team. So tell me, if two out of ten reps can exceed quota then why can't the other eight? There are many reasons for this sad statistic including, but not limited to, poor recruiting and hiring processes, lack of superior sales collateral, non-existent or token-only sales training, etc. I believe that by far the biggest contributing factor to this statistic is simply poor sales management. Without guidance, some reps that are most likely entrepreneurs themselves at heart, figure things out on their own while the rest flounder around scrapping by or waiting to get fired.

The reason I know this is true is because on many occasions after working with a company to implement good sales management, I find that the 80/20 rule seems to no longer apply. When someone is properly wearing the sales manager hat, you will find that the sales revenue numbers from almost every member of the team are clustered close together. They all become the twenty percent!

Keep in mind that sales training should be an ongoing process. Part of the sales manager's job is to keep the sales team informed. The sales team should be some of the first employees to know about product updates, serious bugs, and changes to the roadmap so they are never caught off guard. Competitive updates should be done regularly as well as reviews of new or improved sales collateral.

I would meet once a week with my sales teams as a group and once a week with my team members individually. The group meetings are great for building morale, sharing success stories, reviewing the team's overall performance, and for setting team goals and competitions. The individual meetings provide an opportunity to review a rep's specific activity and sales metrics, discuss stuck sales and to coach as needed. Don't forget to review fundamental sales techniques a few times each year with the team like the ones discussed in the chapter on selling. "Gentlemen, this is a football." Basic blocking and tackling skills need to be sharpened from time to time. In my experience, sales are usually lost not because of some fancy new technique that wasn't learned, but rather because of some very fundamental skill that was forgotten.

Prospecting is different from selling. Selling is all about the perfect placement of facts and benefit statements to a known decision maker. *Prospecting* is the art and process of finding and prequalifying those decision makers so the sales process can begin. I've come to believe that a sales rep who is twice as skilled at prospecting will always outsell the rep who is twice as good at selling. Why? Because it's always easier to *find* hungry people than it is to *make* people hungry. In other words and as I've said before, just showing up at the right place at the right time is over half the battle. You will win zero of the battles you don't show up for. Skillful prospecting is powerful because it significantly increases the probability of showing up at the right time. I talked a lot about lead generation in the section on marketing, so I'm going to focus now on how to train your sales team to follow up on those leads.

Let's assume now that you have a steady stream of leads coming in to distribute to your sales team. They have come from lots of different sources. There's that list of contacts you purchased, responders to your last content offer, web inquires, conference attendees, etc. Prospects will range from a very warm I-want-a-call-back-now kind of lead to a very chilly who-the-hell-are-you *cold* call. Probing questions work well for the former, but the latter requires some technique.

Dale Carnegie once said that if an important person talked to everyone who wanted an audience then that person would not be important for very long. When you call someone who does not know you nor expects your call, you are an interruption. When the phone first rings, you are unknown. You might be a friend or a co-worker so for the first few seconds the individual is all ears. This opportunity should not be squandered. You have about twenty seconds to either live or die so don't waste time with pleasantries or small talk.

The first all-consuming question your prospect will have is "Who is this calling me?" If you don't answer this unvoiced question immediately, then there's a good chance that your prospects will not hear your next few sentences as they ponder various possibilities. If you tell them who you are immediately, then their minds will move quickly to their next question which is, "How do you know about me/get my number?" and then "why are you calling/contacting me?" If you don't offer up this information quickly, then there's a good chance that they won't be listening to the other things you talk about as they continue to speculate. As soon as they know all of these things, the next thought to enter most prospects' minds is, "How can I politely end this interruption." You must get to your value proposition prior to your prospect getting to this question. So never ask if this is a good time to talk or your prospect will jump straight to the last question above.

In the very first twenty seconds you need to communicate three things in rapid succession:

1. Who you are

2. How you got their contact information/why you are calling

3. The most important thing you can do for them or their organization

As soon as you have provided this information you should move to a probing question that is either open ended or one that will generate a "yes" response. For example:

Content requester prospect (*warm* call)

Hello Mr. Jones.
My name is Amanda Smith.
I noticed that you requested our whitepaper/content regarding X.
My job is to assist companies that are considering/evaluating X.
I'm interested to find out what you thought of our paper and if there are any X-related issues with which I might be able to assist you.

Purchased lead prospect (*cold* call)

Hello Mr. Jones.
My name is Amanda Smith.
I saw that you were listed as the X job title/decision maker for your company in [source].
        or - I saw that you attended the X conference, etc.

My job is to assist organizations considering X or to help them with X-related issues.

or - to work with organizations that want to avoid [problem] or get [benefit].

Has your organization ever tried/consider/been concerned about, etc. X-related issue?

Get the prospect engaged in talking with you by quickly communicating your value, expertise, and ability to help. My organization has assisted a number of companies facing X issue or wanting X benefit. Train your team to always start by discussing the business solution or problem rather than your product. Prospects don't care about the drill so discuss their need for holes, the problem of not having good holes, how current hole-creation techniques are too slow, expensive, or inaccurate, etc.

If the prospect throws out an objection to shut you down, then use your objection handling techniques.

We already have a tool that takes care of X.
A lot of my best clients said the same thing before they realized/considered/compared...

If you get your prospect talking, let him or her run. Learn all you can about the company, budget, decision makers, current solution, biases, previous experiences, etc. If you get a *talker* giving you intelligence, keep them going by continuing to ask open-ended probing questions. Take notes as fast as you can type.

If the prospect says that he or she is very busy, up against a deadline, or in a meeting then do not continue. Apologize for the interruption and ask when would be a better time for you to call again. If you are given a date/time, make sure you reference it when you call back,

> *Hi Mr. Jones. This is Amanda Smith again.*
> *When we last spoke you had asked me to call back today concerning..."*

Framing the call back this way will cause the prospect to feel obligated to speak with you. Even though prospects may have simply been trying to get rid of you as quickly as possible, they did ask you to call again at this time so they feel now that they should at least hear you out.

After you've gathered all of the information you can from a prospect about the targeted account and before you spend a lot of time selling, you need to *qualify* the prospect as the right decision maker or at least one of the decision makers for your product or solution. Are you the person in your organization that would evaluate and make purchasing decisions regarding...? *Map* the account. Who else would be involved in this decision? Do you have a budget set aside for this? How soon do you plan to make this decision?

Many times the person you are speaking with is not the decision maker you seek, but he or she may still be a valuable source of information and referrals. So, who would be tasked with evaluating solutions like this? Could you give me his or her number? An *internal referral* really warms up a cold call.

> *Hi Mr. Jones,*
> *My name is Amanda Smith.*
> *Sue Keller suggested that I should give you a call*
> *because...*

The prospect reasons that if Sue referred you, then she must think what you have to say has value.

Don't worry if you aren't getting through to you primary decision makers on your first few calls. In fact, this can be a good thing because it gives you time to gather intelligence that can help you better target your pitch. For example, I was once selling a tool that helped healthcare providers securely communicate patient records. There were dozens of facts and benefits we could state about our product, but after talking to the wrong person at a major hospital chain I learned two important things. First was the guy's name that was most likely the decision maker with the authority and budget to buy my product and the second was that he had just been given a mandate to make sure that all hospital systems were HIPAA privacy compliant. This was a minor benefit of my product, but when I called the decision maker I modified my opening to say, "My job is to help our customers ensure that all of their patient communications are efficient and HIPAA compliant." We talked for nearly an hour and he became one of my biggest accounts.

As with most sales skills, great prospecting has to be practiced and the best practice technique is role-playing. Act it out. Pretend to be the decision maker that each of your reps is calling. After each role-play, ask your team what the role-playing rep did well or miss in the conversation. Part of wearing the sales manager hat is to continuously be sharpening the skills of your team. I would occasionally stand unnoticed and listen to my team members on the phone to assess how they were doing and who might need additional coaching or praise.

I'm not a big fan of hiring an agency to do lead qualification because this approach requires you to forfeit a lot of the control that makes a great sales manager worth his or her weight in gold. In the early days, you need to hear the objections first hand to perfect your product and pitch. If you do use an agency, make sure you give them a proven script to use and a detailed definition of what a qualified lead is, especially if you are paying them on a per-lead basis. Otherwise, your sales team could waste a lot of time presenting to unqualified leads.

The final responsibility I want to touch on regarding the sales manager hat is that of a cheerleader. Sales and particularly prospecting can be grueling and demoralizing. Prospects can be cruel and demeaning to your team while doing their job. Always keep this in mind and try to keep spirits up amongst your team. Position yourself as a mentor who hungers for their individual success, rather than a taskmaster cracking the whip. Celebrate every victory publicly. Constantly encourage your team. I know you can do this! I believe in you! Yes we lost that one, but brush it off and get back on the horse. You got this!

Having your team members share both good and bad experiences together in the group meeting can be very encouraging. Remind your team that they are professionals and to try to enjoy the thrill of the chase. Games are only fun if they present us with a challenge that we must overcome. If a game is not challenging, then we quickly lose interest.

My father loves fishing more than any person I've ever known. I've seen him patiently circle my lake for hours casting his line and catching nothing on a cold day. He patiently keeps working his process changing lures, location, speed, depth, and dozens of other subtle variables I've yet to fully understand. Eventually, he always seems to pull one in no matter how harsh the conditions or how long it takes. He explained it to me once. *The true fisherman does not begrudge each cast that does not produce a fish. It's all part of the joy of fishing.*

Remind your team to enjoy the process and its challenges. Make it a game. If you've prepared them well and given them the tools and encouragement they need, then success never seems further away then the next cast.

The Leader's Hat

I believe there is a big difference between wearing the manager's hat and wearing the leader's hat. Stephen Covey illustrated this concept brilliantly when he said that *management* is like providing the tools, process, and plans to most efficiently get teams to cut down trees. Whereas *leadership* is the guy who climbs the highest tree and yells, "Wrong forest"!

I often tell my founders that if they expertly manage the wrong things, then their team members will simply do them faster all day long. Managers ensure that a team has the training and resources necessary to get a job done and they monitor that process to ensure that the job really is getting done. By contrast, the first responsibility in wearing the leader's hat is to provide clear strategic direction. You have to be the one to ensure that your managers have all been tasked with managing things that are going to ultimately move your company in the direction it needs to go. When you slide this hat on, it's time to think about the big picture. Pull your head out of operations and stop thinking about tactics, efficiencies, and process improvement. Instead, start thinking about your overall strategic direction. While wearing this hat everything is on the table for consideration. Leaders don't think about how to sell more widgets. They ask themselves if they should even be selling widgets any longer.

Successful startup entrepreneurs have to have both a microscope and a telescope in their pocket at all times. Most people gravitate to one or the other, but not entrepreneurs. When I invest in a founder, I always look for those people that can drill down on very specific problems and details when they need to, but then are able to instantly zoom way back out to see how that smallest part fits into the overall big scheme. This way of thinking is a must. If you stay at the big picture level, then you won't be able to build all of the little parts you need to fulfill that vision. However, if you always keep your head down in the details then you are certain to lose your way. You have to constantly be looking at the stars and then back at your sails, ropes, and pulleys before looking back at the stars again to accomplish both navigation and propulsion simultaneously.

I always tried to get my senior management teams to stop thinking tactically at least once a month and take the time to help me think strategically. This can be a real challenge in the heat of day-to-day battles. Sometimes I'd invite them to my home or beach house to get them away from the disruptions of the office and the patterns of office thinking. I would facilitate the discussion by asking open-ended questions. Have our experiences this month confirmed or caused us to question our target market, sales strategy, product roadmap, etc.? What are our competitors doing differently and why are they doing that? Is this still the industry where we should be focused?

The Startup Hats

The art of strategic leadership is to question everything. Big companies have more people, more technology, and more resources than a startup. Our only advantage is that we can innovate, try things, and change direction hundreds of times faster than large organizations. Leaders push their teams to contemplate, iterate, learn, modify, and re-apply as quickly as possible because in a startup, this is our biggest advantage and most powerful weapon.

I love reading books about great leaders, the problems they faced, and how they navigated crisis. Andy Grove, the iconic CEO of Intel®, knew what it meant to wear the leader's hat. Intel was and always had been in the business of making memory chips. This is what built the company and made them successful, but when foreign competition started flooding their market with cheap memory chips, Grove could see the writing on the wall. He was famous for saying, "only the paranoid survive". He called his management team together and asked, "If the board decided to fire us all and bring in a new management team tomorrow, what would those guys do?" This was Grove's way of getting his team to rethink everything from a fresh new perspective. It was a radical move, but under Grove's leadership, Intel stopped making memory chips all together and started making processors for personal computers. The rest is history.

Leaders know there are no guarantees. The very thing that made you successful last year might be the very thing that causes your downfall in the next year.

Some view the leader's hat as a crown because of the authority it represents, but good leaders are far from dictators. Good leaders are consensus builders. They are thoughtful and seek out opposing opinions. They genuinely want to understand all points of view especially those different from their own. They take the time to socialize important decisions and welcome critiques of their thought process. Leaders are often unsure of what to do. They are painfully aware of the consequences of making mistakes. So they take their time to gather all the data they can get and all the opinions and counsel before making the hard calls.

Some of the startup hats are what I call *fast hats* while others are *slow hats*. The sales hat is certainly a fast hat fully equipped with wind goggles. When you have this hat on, you want to make as many contacts as you can as quickly as possible. Check off those follow up calls and flap your wings furiously if you want to get airborne. The same goes for administrative work. Do it just good enough to get by and as quickly as possible. Other hats are slow hats like recruiting and most certainly *leadership*.

When it's time to slip on your leadership hat, it's going to feel very inefficient and time consuming. This is another of those startup paradoxes where fast is slow and slow is fast. I assure you that if you try to get leadership done quickly, then you will most likely be rethinking, repairing and redoing the same thing all over again. Take your time. Socialize ideas and gather all the feedback and viewpoints you can. Sit still and ponder all of the viewpoints and data you collect. Sleep on it. Ask more questions. Knee jerk leadership is not leadership at all. Take the time that big decisions deserve.

There are lots of ways to screw up wearing the leader's hat. The most common fashion blunder I see occurs when the crown slips down over the leaders' eyes. Like kings of old, they mistakenly think that "might makes right". Since I have the crown, I'll just make a quick and efficient decision without taking the time to gather feedback or to see how others interpret the same data. They see only one point of view, their own. I'm too embarrassed to illustrate this point using one of the many sad examples I can recall from my early attempts at leadership, but trust me when I say that the best path is rarely seen with just one pair of eyes.

Those not wearing the leadership hat properly often make under informed decisions. Even when they do find themselves on the right path and look back, no one is whole heartily following them because their team had no part in helping to create that vision.

When you close your eyes and try to picture a leader, what do you see? If your image is of someone talking, then think again. Great leaders spend far more time *listening* than talking. They must hear, understand, and contemplate many different perspectives before issuing just one mandate.

So you have to be humble to wear this hat, but you also have to have tremendous self-confidence. I've seen would be leaders that were afraid to ask for the counsel of others because they feared that this would make them appear stupid or someone who does not know what to do. Well guess what? Leaders often don't know what to do and are uncertain of which path to take. It is the fact that you acknowledge what you don't know that makes you a good leader. Ironically, your team will hold you in greater esteem for this honesty. Get it out of your head that you have to always be right to be the leader. You don't have to be and you won't. What makes you a leader is that you understand and honor the process that statistically will lead your organization to the highest probability of well-informed decision-making.

The worst way of all to wear the leader's hat is to just put it on partially. I've worked with star decision-makers who could wear the hat to make the easy calls, but who just could not keep it on when the decisions that had to be made got really difficult. Indecisiveness is a bigger problem than arrogance when wearing this hat because the arrogant leader, who blunders ahead without counsel or forethought, will occasionally stumble onto the right path. Leaders who freeze in their tracks in the face of a daunting decision can paralyze their organizations. They just keep waiting for more information and for the correct path to become more obvious. Remember that making no decision is to make a decision. It's OK to let some big decisions simmer for a while, but ultimately almost any direction is better than no direction at all. The right decision might be to go down a certain path for a finite period of time and then reassess. It's OK to launch temporary initiatives and explore. Moving forward is a must for a startup because your resource clock is ticking and most often it is the things that we learn while groping forward that give us the information we need to perfect our future decision-making.

Leaders have to be courageous. It's not easy making high-risk decisions with limited information, but that's your job. You know full well that the outcome of your decision in a few months may make you look like an idiot or the smartest guy in world, but you know that neither of these is true. You are just the person who had to make the call and you did your job as best you could with the information you could get at the time. You are the leader because someone has to be. Others have the luxury of second guessing decisions and being Monday morning quarterbacks but not the leader. They are not afraid to make mistakes once they've done their best to make the right call. As CEO of my companies, I can think of numerous really bad decisions I made, but we survived and learned and eventually flourished. Sometimes when I'm consoling one of my CEO founders sitting in the full realization of the consequences of a really bad call, I tell them this. If you did your homework, sought out every view point, and made the best decision you could with the information you had available at the time, then that's all you can do. You did your job. Right or wrong, be proud of that because it took courage.

Besides thinking strategically, building consensus and making the hard calls, another important component of leadership relates to your authority and its preservation. As I've said, good leaders encourage differing opinions and debate, but once a decision is made, the leader should tolerate nothing but full and enthusiastic adherence to his or her mandate. Debate must come to an end. Companies can't thrive without a respected chain of command that ends with a strong leader at the top. Even when you can't bring the troops to a consensus, decisions still have to be made. Getting everyone to pull in the same direction, even if that direction is less than perfect, is always better than having a fragmented team pulling in different directions and bickering among themselves.

The rank and file employees always need to feel that management is united behind the stated direction and strategy. Building a startup is like going to war. The stakes may not be as high as life and limb, but they often do include hearth and home. Imagine the general yelling "charge" on the battle field while various line commanders tell their troops, "I told the general that this was a bad time to charge." or "I think we'd do better to advance slowly". Some troops advance, other stay behind and the battle is lost. When leadership is perceived as weak, various individuals or groups within your company may not take ownership of the direction or do their part to see it through. They will continue to campaign for what they thought was better, complain about the current path and those supporting it, and even in some cases actively sabotage its success to prove their point.

People will always be tugging at your leadership hat to see if it comes off. It is just human nature to test the limits of your own power and influence. As the leader, you have to make it perfectly clear that once your decision is made that it is final. You expect one hundred percent enthusiastic adherence to the stated plan because anything less is treason. On many occasions, after listening to my management team hotly debate a big decision without reaching a consensus, I would make the final call. After which, I would always remind them of my expectations.

> *Thank you all for helping me make this difficult decision. I know you are all so passionate about this because you care deeply and I appreciate that. Now that I have made the decision, I expect every one of you to support it as if it were your own idea. No one outside of this room should even know who held what viewpoint during our debates. As far as they are concerned, this decision was unanimous.*

And that is how it has to go. I would excuse my captains for making mistakes and screwing up as they experimented and tried new things, but there was never a second warning when it came to treason.

Insubordination is a lesser offence that if left unchecked, always leads to treason. Insubordination is when someone openly disrespects you or challenges your authority. Although toeing the line, they grumble, make a negative public comment or in some other way show their displeasure or disagreement with the decision you have made. This should never be tolerated. When someone comes to you privately and constructively suggesting that

201

you reconsider something in light of new data not previously discussed, this is not insubordination. You will know disrespect when you see it and like a stage-three cancer you had better be ready to act quickly. If others see you tolerate insubordination and do nothing, then the new norm in your company will be that insubordination is OK at all levels. This is the beginning of the end of your ability to lead. No company can thrive without a respected chain of command anchored by strong leadership at the top.

Almost all of my first time startup CEO's have struggled with firing team members even after repeated offenses of which any one of them should have been more than enough cause. They often feel guilty and make excuses for the offending or non-performing person. The problem has almost always spread to others in their young company before they realize how serious it is. The proverb of one bad apple spoiling the entire bunch has been around since ancient times because each generation rediscovers its wisdom. As unpleasant as it is, an occasional firing can be a good thing for your organization. There's nothing like heads rolling in the parking lot to snap everyone back in line. It communicates that you are serious about the chain of command and what you expect of your managers.

At the first hint of insubordination, call the offending employee into your office or some other private place and express in no uncertain terms your displeasure in what you are detecting. If the first offense is small I'd just give a stern warning, "Do you feel that you are unable to enthusiastically support my decisions?" Let them squirm for a minute. If they try to restate their argument, cut them off by saying that this is not about that. That decision has already been made. This discussion is about their inability to support a directive. End with a warning, "I cannot tolerate this, so if I hear of or even sense the slightest hint of insubordination from you or concerning you from anyone else, I will be forced to dismiss you for cause." Am I clearly understood?

Remember that as a leader you don't have to be liked, but you do have to be respected. Everyone carrying the authority and burden of the leader's hat has to deal with insubordination at some point and how decisively you deal with it, will define your future effectiveness as a leader. You will have a lot less problem with insubordination if your managers feel that you take the time to really listen to them and understand their viewpoints and concerns prior to making your decisions. If you make decisions in a vacuum, then you are in a sense disrespecting your team by dismissing their expertise and frontline experience. Don't be surprised if that disrespect comes home to roost.

Teams really support and get excited about their own ideas, so try to give credit to others even for your own ideas. Keep asking leading questions until your team comes up with your idea *on their own*. People are so supportive and emotionally attached to their own ideas. Remember that people tend to only support ideas that they had a hand in creating or shaping, so always try to use the ideas of others when possible.

There is another marquee leadership quality. Leaders are confident. This is not the confidence of always being right but rather the confidence that they know what their job is as a leader and that they are doing it correctly. Leaders must trust themselves, the decision making process, and their judgment. Some entrepreneurs are always looking to a board member or advisor to make the decision for them. It does not help that some advisors view themselves as the source of all wisdom and actually take offence when entrepreneurs disagree with their counsel or choose to go a different direction.

My advice to you is to trust yourself. I know what it's like. You live your startup every single day. You think about it as you fall asleep each night. In a short time, you will have sat through hundreds of meetings and witnessed firsthand the exact moment when a prospect's eyebrow raised or forehead wrinkled when something was said. No advisor is living this the way you are. You are the best and most qualified person to make the hard calls in your business. I challenge my entrepreneurs. I ask them to review the metrics. I may even tell them a sad story about how I once screwed up doing something similar, but in the end I encourage each entrepreneur to go with his or her gut. Listen to all wise counsel and debate the hell out of important decisions, but then make the call that feels right to you even if you can't explain exactly why. Regardless, once you make that call, it's the right call and any advisor or board member worth his or her salt will honor and support that decision.

The Startup Hats

The leadership hat is also equipped with a built-in megaphone because leading is not just about making big decisions. It is also about taking the time to communicate those decisions to your troops. Startups are always experimenting and trying new things to see what works. Change is the only constant. Entrepreneurs are usually far more comfortable with change then the general population. We can review the facts and quickly become comfortable with a new direction or approach, but where we usually screw up is in how we roll change out to our people. The rank and file staff will not have had the time that you have had to review all the data and wise council. This is where *change management* is critical. A leader knows that most people don't deal well with change. They fear the unknown and want the normalcy of predictability. When a change is called for, the leader has to take the time to get his or her organization comfortable with the move. If you turn the wheel of the bus too sharply, then team members can get slung out the windows in the process. Heading in the right direction is little consolation if you lose your team in the process. Leadership is not only about course adjustments, but also how to systematically and thoughtfully implement those adjustments.

I encourage my startup CEO's to over communicate with their managers and employees. Explain to your troops why certain decisions are being made and how important each of their roles relate to the success of the new strategy or direction. Take the time to send out company update emails discussing goals, celebrating individual and group successes, and explaining why a particular change is important. When staff members feel left in the dark they start to feel unimportant. With the absence of real facts, employees can start to imagine the worst. When the CEO takes the time to communicate with the troops, the staff feels that their leader really values them. In a startup, usually full speed is the right speed, but not when it comes to change management. Slowing down to navigate a curve with your team is not inefficient. It's the only smart way to make a sharp turn.

This may sound like it contradicts some things I've said previously, but leadership is also about focus and staying the course. It's true that much of your success in a startup will come from quickly trying different things and seeing what works, but this has to start settling down some as your venture matures. You can't keep chasing every shinny object. Good enough is often good enough. In other words, leaders have to know how to say "no".

It is often said that *lack of focus* is the primary reason startups fail. I don't say that because it makes entrepreneurs afraid to try new things, but it is true that much of what you do as the leader is to referee scarce resource allotments. Leaders know that everything you say "yes" to means that you'll have to say "no" to something else. Therefore, they are always thinking in terms of *opportunity costs* i.e. the cost of not doing the next best option. It is good that you have created a culture of risk taking and that you have demonstrated your openness to new ideas and suggestions, but the counter balance to this is the need to occasionally reign in this flow of experimentation.

Your managers will constantly be approaching you asking for more resources or for your approval to pursue some new cool initiative. You'll want to say "yes". I always hated to throw cold water on the enthusiasm of one of my team members, but leaders have to keep an eye on the big picture and limited resources. There are a lot of shinny objects and latest fads to chase. A top sales guy may want you to buy a list of contacts in the financial services space so he or she can test that new market's demand for your offering. Your product manager or lead developer is next in line to speak with you. Just because one company did well with a unique new user interface, doesn't mean that you should immediately rewrite your interface to resemble it. A leader is constantly asking, "Is this core to our business strategy and primary value propositions?" Is it a "must have" or just a "nice to have". If you aren't saying "no" a lot of the time then your business will run the risk of being a mile wide and only an inch deep.

You can help a disappointed manager understand your reasoning by pulling out the product roadmap or list of approved company initiatives and ask which one should be taken off the list to free up the time and capital needed for this new initiative. Remember that you don't have to always say "no". Much of the time you can just say "not now". It's not a bad idea. It's just one that we don't have the resources to implement at this time.

There's one last thing I need to say about the leader's hat. It also comes with a built-in spotlight. Everyone in the company is always observing a leader. For this reason, they are thoughtful and careful with what they say and how they act. Leaders are mindful of their promises. They think about things before they respond because they know that they are often establishing policy or at least precedence when they answer a seemingly innocuous question from one of their troops.

This is an area of leadership where I had much to learn. I had to apologize to an employee once for saying something without thinking about its impact. I jokingly suggested to a group gathered in a hallway a course of action that inadvertently would have dramatically impacted his commission-based income. For days he worried about how he would deal with this eventuality financially and he even almost dropped his child's private school enrollment. I'll never forget what he said to me, "Everything you say carries a lot of weight". If you are the leader, then in some respects you are the one holding the very livelihoods of your employees and their families in your hand as well as a good chunk of their self-esteem. To be in such a position should be viewed as a sacred trust. It is a huge responsibility and one that should never be taken lightly.

People want to believe that they are following a leader who cares about more than just making money. They want to know that your goals also include helping to develop your team and your employees' general well being. They'd like to think that there are some things you'd never do and ways you'd never act, even if it meant forfeiting much of your own personal success. People are always observing their leader hoping to find clues that these things are true and that we are indeed worthy of their loyalty. They see how we treat that person about to be let go. They see how we honor our business agreements and how we treat our partners and they rightfully conclude that we will treat them no better. The leader that people want to follow is the one who sometimes takes a stand and says, "We don't do business that way here."

When dealing with my employees, I applied a simple three-question test before doing things that I knew would impact them. Answering these questions honestly often changed my mind from a course of action or at least the way I intended to go about it.

1.   *Is it necessary?*
2.   *Is it fair?*
3.   *Is it kind?*

The leader is viewed as the heart of the company; the one person who more than anyone else represents the values that make up the corporate culture. Climbing the face of the mountain is hard and it should make you a little callused, but never ruthless. Winning at all cost is not winning at all. So while in the fray, you have to make sure that you don't forget that who you are is different from the job you do. Long after your job is done, you will still have to live with you and the path of blessings or destruction in your wake.

Remember that people admire competence, but they follow integrity. For much of my career I have tried to define what integrity really means. I have come to believe that integrity is what happens when what you say you are, believe and value, all perfectly line up with what you actually do. In other words, integrity only manifests itself through our actions. It is our actions that define us, not what we say we are or say we believe. In truth, our actions are the only window to the soul showing our true nature. If you want to know what kind of leader you are, then look to your actions. Likewise, if you want to be a different kind of leader, every decision is an opportunity to prove to yourself and your people the better person you have become.

I don't plan on waxing too philosophical in a business how-to book, but I can tell you this. Many years from now, when you reflect on all the sound and fury of your ventures, you won't tend to dwell so much on the big mistakes or even the perfectly executed maneuvers, but you will spend a lot of time thinking about the people who took those journeys with you and how you treated them.

Conclusion

I read an article once about a man who decided to interview hundreds of people on their deathbeds. One of the questions he asked was, "What do you regret most about your life?" I don't remember the top things on the list, but I do remember being struck by the realization that what people tend to regret the most are not the things they did, but rather the things they had hoped to do but did not.

To those of you who accept the challenge to live a life less ordinary, my hat is off to you. I hope you shape your ventures well and that they in turn do the same for you. Win or lose, it really is all about that journey. I hope this book helps you avoid many of the mistakes I made and I hope that you are a faster learner and better listener than me. Most of all, I wish you no regrets.

Made in the USA
Charleston, SC
04 April 2015